SACRED P[ATHS] ENTWINED

Gill Potter

Seek the perfection of your mission

To Lynn.

Love & best wishes

Gill Potter

xx.

SACRED PATHS ENTWINED

First published in 2012 by
Ecademy Press
48 St Vincent Drive, St Albans, Herts, AL1 5SJ
info@ecademy-press.com
www.ecademy-press.com

Printed and bound by Lightning Source in the UK and USA

Designed by Julie Oakley

Printed on acid-free paper from managed forests. This book is printed on demand, so no copies will be remaindered or pulped.

ISBN 978-1-908746-29-0

A CIP catalogue record for this book is available from the British Library.

This book is available online and in all good bookstores.

Dedication

I dedicate this book to all families in the hope for greater understanding, forgiveness and love.

For Zoe

Life supports life!

Acknowledgements

Sacred Paths Entwined is my spiritual memoir and a guide to unlock your sacred path and purpose. It is based on my real life experiences*. Its main purpose is to enlighten, enchant and awaken you to the divine within you. Understanding how we are all one and connected is the reason for the title.

For my parents Maureen and Ian who gave me the gift of life and allowed me to experience divine love, faith and grace. I am grateful for everything in my life and pray that in reading my story you will be filled with these qualities too, to support you in seeking the perfection of your mission!

I would also like to thank Caroline Myss and everyone at CMED (Caroline Myss Education Institute). My international Lollipop crew Clare Willocks, Valerie Rene Sheppard, Kim Richardson, Mary Dillon, who I met in Chicago in May 2009, Bernadette Doyle, *Damsels in Success*, Sanaya Roman, Duane Packer (channels for Orin & Daben), Christina Morassi, Beth Benton, Jen Barber, Pam Robertson, Stan Giles and Dan Bradbury. You have all been integral to my journey.

Thank YOU for being a part of my sacred path and for reading my story.

Namaste!

*Some names have been changed.

Praise for this book

Gill Potter is quite a unique storyteller and she takes the reader on a real rollercoaster of emotion. She lays bare her life and invites you into her darkest times, and does not pull any punches when describing her pain and sadness.

However, the book is also a mixture of textbook, poetry, and autobiography with an introduction to various topics such as Sacred Contracts and astrology, which leave the reader wanting to know more. The poetry throughout is very beautiful, and describes each aspect of the story in just the right way.

Gill's story is powerful, encouraging, and shows what faith and opening up of the heart can do to serve us in this life.

Karen Edgar, Founder – Smart Woman Academy

I loved learning about Gill's story; it was fascinating and a very brave thing to do, to open your heart and soul for others to read. I have had a real interest in astrology since I was young and have dipped in and out over the years, so I really enjoyed reading more about it. I am also working with Gill on casting my Sacred Contract, which has been a fabulous process so far. I look forward to completing it with Gill.

Lyn Bromley, Managing Director – First Impressions Training Limited

I really enjoyed reading about Gill's own personal journey; her struggles, and how she discovered her truth. As someone who has had a passing interest in astrology over the years, I have gained new insights from how Gill weaves her experiences of astrology and Sacred Contracts into her story. I have also cast my own Sacred Contract with Gill, and it has brought new realisations about my own life purpose.

Sue M. Gylman, Alternative Success – Business Support Network for Therapists.

A story of an inspiring journey that will make you question your own sacred path.

Zoe Brockman, Student of French and economics, Canterbury University, Kent.

Gill offers a deeply personal and authentic account of her own sacred path, and a world of factual detail about how to discover and follow yours.

Rev. Becky Jones – Interfaith Minister and Spiritual Counsellor www.authenticspirit.co.uk

Contents

Preface

Have you ever felt you had a tale to tell and that what you have learned needs to be shared with a wider audience? My tale is more of a family dynasty/blockbuster but it is not set in the world of high finance, power or glamorous lifestyles. Instead, the inverse is true – it is a true story of powerlessness, shame, and fear of facing the truth – my truth and following my calling! They say the truth will set you free, but in the process, you have to face everything that is not truth. Moreover, if truth equates to love, then this is MY STORY of love – DIVINE LOVE!

What follows is an account of my life and my sacred purpose. Love and truth will stretch you to the very limits, crack open your heart and allow the divine to flow through you. My Charism is to tell the truth, to honour the truth, to live by it and to die for it too if need be! I cannot live any other way! I watch people lie or tell half-truths, brush past pain as if it is a fly in their soup, or cross the street and pretend they do not see! When we do that we live a lie, we collude in the illusion and we allow stories to form that perpetrate the lies for the sake of money, security, peace and personal comfort. In the end, though, we all have to face the truth.

As M Scott Peck says in *People of the Lie* – each of us holds the key to healing human evil by participating in seeking only truth for the sake of truth and to serve the divine plan in that quest. My first love was learning the secrets that would shape my life path – family secrets of illegitimacy, adoption and shame. These patterns can wreak havoc on the psyche and are brushed under carpets to keep those who are containers for them powerless and lacking in self-worth. The worst fear being that when the can of worms eventually opens, then everyone who is involved will be seen in their lowest or highest light! It can be a big burden to carry generational energies but also a great honour! For those of us with such a badge of 'honour' we are called to carry it as our shame/our cross, and so part of my mission was to discover why this had been my Sacred Contract for this lifetime. I had this psychic stamp invisibly tattooed on me even while I was in my mother's womb. Although all seemed normal at my birth, I always knew this lifetime was to learn about power and being powerless in a world that would undergo a tremendous transformation in my lifetime!

Prologue

Two huge black eyes gazed up at them all, while taking in her new surroundings. It had been a quick, easy labour, and the four faces that gazed back lovingly could never comprehend what this child carried within... It was a perfect, crisp, moonlit night and the baby was a wonderful early Christmas gift for the family. December 15th 1965, and all seemed well for the happy family. A new addition to give them and their two longed-for children a perfect Christmas day. All seemed to be very conventional at this moment and little did they know of what she would live through during her lifetime. The new parents held the baby, cooing lovingly, and still unsure of which name to choose. The new arrival had taken some time to be conceived, almost as if the exact time and date had been chosen with great precision and love.

It was just after 3 a.m. as the content grandparents waved goodbye and headed home. The new baby, Gillian Moir Potter, had arrived safe and sound, at 1.35 a.m. in a small two-bedroom flat in Westwood, East Kilbride.

I Am

I am from a country of beauty
That is yet to find itself
A family who have suffered
Holding secrets and hopes and dreams
Deeply inside
Of loss and fear
Of joy and sorrow

I am from
The Source of all life
The deepest ocean
The widest river
The rustling leaves
And
The Oak tree that stands proud
The richest treasure and the blackest coal face – inert yet vibrant
Glistening and sparkling like new jewels awaiting inspection

I am from
The formed and the formless
The insider and the non-conformist The love and the hate
The sweetest taste of summer
Like rain on your face
That falls in harmony with
The greatness of God and
Opens your heart to all that has been and all that will be

I am from
The life that gives life
The dream that becomes reality
The despair that can be joy
And the love that transforms the past!

Chapter 1

WE ARE ALL ONE

I love the interconnection
The symbolic knowing
The meaning behind the words
The unsaid verse
The hidden joy
The sorrow that must be owned
The lightness of a bright day
The sweetest music
The hearts that can open
The language of the inner voice
The soul's path and the sacred purpose
That binds it altogether
As One!

Following my yellow brick road

It all started on Hogmanay (or old year's night as it is sometimes called in Scotland) when I knew something had to change and big time. I wanted to change my life in 2009 and really connect with what I felt sure in my heart I was here to do.

However, the question was how to do it?

I had tried so many things and explored so many paths; I had some success for sure and enough to keep me on the look out for the next step; however, I felt that something big was needed to really shake my life up, as it felt stuck! I had lost my Dad and my grandfather in 2008, so it had been a very emotional time for me. I felt empty inside, and knew that there must be more to my life than what seemed to be my fate at that moment!

Therefore, I enrolled on a business course called Alchemy, and as soon as I clicked submit, I felt an inner call to contact David Smith at CMED in Chicago, to see if I could do the Sacred Contracts course. I had been familiar with Caroline Myss's work since 1998 when it virtually saved my life – no kidding! On January 1st 2009, I sent an e-mail to David, who is Caroline Myss's business partner, asking about the course.

I had thought of doing the course before but this time I had a strong intuitive hunch to do so.

Little did I know that my life was about to change... as I followed my own yellow brick road listening to the call of my Spirit.

Therefore, to cut a very long story short, that one decision activated my own Sacred Contract, And of that, I am absolutely certain!

This book is about that journey I have been on and how we are connected – in fact, how all sacred paths are entwined, and more importantly, how to understand and light up your own sacred path!

So how did I end up going to Chicago and working with Caroline Myss? Well, the first book I read by Caroline Myss was called *Why people don't heal and how they can* back in 1998. It came into my possession due to intense guidance to go to the bookshop. I had come through a difficult few weeks of deep despair and was really looking at why I was not getting any better from the health issues I had at this time. I had just had some cranio-sacral therapy, and went through a very intense 'confession' with the therapist. I really felt that it was time to clear out the ghosts from my past and negative attitudes and beliefs that I had held, which I realised did not serve me anymore. In fact en route to meet her, I remember thinking, "this is the last chance saloon for me!" I realised that it was time to let go and almost immediately, the magic of healing seemed to enter my life.

It was the next day that I remember – as if 'told' – to go to the bookstore. "Oh no, not another book," I thought to myself, feeling that I needed another book like a hole in the head. So many books surrounded me at my small flat, all of which had been my daily companions whilst on my quest for inner healing; yet little did I know that this next one was going to be the catalyst that would change my life and sense of healing forever.

I arrived at Waterstone's – and the book that I had been compelled to find – literally flew from the shelf. The title connected with me (of course), and so I opened it and read the first sentence: "In the late spring of 1988, I arrived at the Findhorn Community in north-eastern Scotland, to teach a healing workshop." That one sentence told me that this was why I was in the bookshop that day. I had become unwell in 1988 (a year that my life changed forever), lived in Scotland and knew of Findhorn, having always wanted to visit it and was desperately seeking guidance on how to heal what seemed to me an unhealable condition (wound). Therefore, it was the answer to my prayers, and it started me on a new road towards health and wholeness.

Finding peace amid chaos

"Pay more attention to your spirit than to your body when healing is required. Inspiration will activate your spirit more than any other quality. So feed it in times of need with inspirational stories that will invoke it." C Myss

In January 1998, I made the decision to keep a spiritual diary, on the inner prompting of my soul. I had heard of the idea firstly whilst studying soul-centred astrology, but had not got round to putting it into practise! You see, I felt like a victim – a victim of this illness that controlled my life – a victim of all the events that seemed to have brought me to this point. Therefore, it was a very disempowering situation, as you can imagine. My self-esteem was at rock bottom, and although I had studied astrology for many years, the light and the healing that I sought appeared to be driving me to my knees, which would eventually take me to this point of great surrender and transformation into a new life!

Rather than keep putting off the inevitable and feeling like something within me needed to be expressed, I decided to buy and start writing a spiritual diary. I purchased a blue hardback notebook with a teddy bear on the front, which was to become my daily companion – a place to write out my grief, release the ghosts from the past and address issues that for me seemed to have no answers. Perhaps this new medium would afford me an answer. This was my barely uttered prayer.

On the first page, I wrote my intention – to record my thoughts, feelings, ideas and spiritual occurrences, which I felt needed to be divulged on paper. Since then, my diary has always been for my eyes only; however, I now feel it is time to share that journey with you, in the hope that it will help someone else. In truth, this journal became a record of my own personal journey from darkness into the light. 1998 was the year that lifted me to a place of unification with the divine within me! If my journey and the subsequent understanding of my own path and purpose can help others who are in despair (as I was that year), then I am very happy to do so!

I began writing my spiritual journal in January 1998 when I was 32 years old.

For ten years I was severely and chronically unwell (the previous six years, 1992–1998 had seen my once vibrant health become progressively worse), and I was on the slippery slope to oblivion.

The worst symptom was the pain and in addition, the knowledge that each time I attempted to overcome this by moving beyond the boundary

I felt comfortable and safe in, I would often suffer days of severe pain, inability to sleep, nausea, nightmares and breathing difficulties. This all resulted in me being controlled by fear – in fact, it was terror. Terror of what my life had become, and a feeling of helplessness that I would never be able to change it for the better.

This is one of the first entries. I wrote it after being out for an afternoon and expressed my fear of what the night may bring. Obviously, the early entries are coming from the darkness – but how can we ever truly know the light if we cannot face our own and others' darkness? This is why the bigger picture is required rather than one isolated piece of our life. That will become apparent as I write and describe the journey that followed. Some of it is quite raw – as I say, I wrote it to help me heal, and therefore it was not intended to be an art form.

21/1/1998

A bitter day

Bitterness unyielding rises up in me,
Eating up every decent word, thought, action
I've ever performed – for what?
To suffer this nightmare of unending days and nights.
Writhing in agony, scared to breathe or sleep for fear of what
tomorrow brings.
It's in the past – that's for sure!
Nausea, tight screaming pain and a brain like a sponge
I cling on to every, last bitter breath of the past, cos I know the
future only too well
Hell, hell, and more hell!
Who cares about my hell
Who knows how it feels
To be unable to tell
The endless symptoms of pain that yell
You're nothing –
You're better off dead than living this daily diet of fear and
pain and despair!
Only to be slapped in the face

Be positive, pretend you're well
Put it behind you and start anew
If only it was all so easy
In the glossy packaged, hard sell
To be free and feel the wind on my face
As I turn with joy to race
The moon, the sun and the stars
Great symbols of a better world
I taste the sweet essence as I escape from the hell of ME
Or even the hell of being ME!

Catharsis

As I wrote each poem – or piece of prose – a catharsis occurred, and as such, years on and having a wealth of understanding and realisations about who I truly am along with my purpose in life, afforded me a degree of insight that my unconscious was attempting to communicate with me. So often, it seems, secrets are hidden inside of us – blocked and repressed – to try to keep us safe or to protect others. However, they are no longer appropriate mediums for us – this is an illustration of that of course – just the ego's way of attempting to control the soul and insist that we are separate from our true divinity, to keep it from succumbing to the divine.

Often, once we start writing and expressing ourselves fully, there is a most wonderful release. This occurs partly because we are no longer in denial and have chosen to face our demons. It takes courage and determination to live your life purposefully and know your highest potential. So many will say "You are living your life purpose by being alive" but the whole point of knowing you are in the fullest expression of it is the fact that you do feel so wonderfully and amazingly alive and fulfilled by each moment – even the difficult ones. There is then, no more hiding or pretending. No more secrets of shame or blame or unspoken criticisms. We stop judging others and that allows us to feel less judged and more loved.

22/1/98

A brighter Day

New hope awakens in me today
As I feel brighter and able to begin again
Gone is the bitterness and fear of yesterday I
feel freshly cleansed by the new day
Sweet tender hope
Fragile to touch and delicate to taste
I breathe it in joyfully and know I can cope
With whatever lies ahead
Good, bad or indifferent
New strength and vitality
Fill me with the will to hope
For a better, brighter day ahead
And the knowledge that no longer do I wish I was dead!
I can be free again
Like the moon, the stars and the sun I dream of in the night
That keep me happy and feel alright!

Adieu!

So it was this dark night of the soul journey that would throw up all my unanswered questions and make me really look at my life from a new perspective. I discovered in this process that no one need ever be in despair – there is always hope and miracles never cease, no matter how bad life can seem at times!

What you deny you declare. What you declare you create. Acceptance of something places you in control of it. That which you deny you cannot control, for you have said it is not there. Therefore, what you deny controls you.

24/1/98

Tick Tock

Tick Tock says the clock
Bringing another day to an end
Some days are long and slow
While others speed by in the blink of an eye
What have I done today I think aloud
Incarcerated in my home which doubles
As a prison in bad days
More chained and restricted than
Any prisoner in gaol could imagine
By an all-engulfing illness, which ties me up and leaves me
screaming
For a quick release in view of time served
Ten years have almost passed
Since I saw my illness reflected back
In an image of fear and distress and confusion
As slowly I began to realise
Something had started to change
Slowly insidiously like that tick tock
Of the living room clock I knew life could never be the same
At first I thought I could cope
Be in control and hold myself together
But slowly I felt the clamp tighten
The pain increase and a flood of symptoms
Duly overwhelm my body, mind and peace
I tried to explain, to search for a cause
But I soon realised no one else could see
The changes going on inside of me
So I retreated further and tried my best
To suppress and stem this tidal wave
Self-denial and fear were the tests I tried to pass – but in vain
And now I look back
And count all the days and nights since passed
Slowly at times and then quick as a flash

23, 24, 25, 26, 27, 28, 29, 30, 31 – these years all gone!
Lost years, painful years
Sorrow-filled years
But they are in the past now
And I hope that one day soon I will look at the clock
And see a new image emerge
And a new time when I can talk
Of new beginnings and close the chapter
Of these ten years and mark it – the past!

30/1/98

My Guide appears

After writing the last piece, TICK TOCK, I began reading a self-help book called *Be Your Own Counsellor* and did the first exercise, which connected me to my guide. I was very surprised to discover he was a man and he told me he would help me develop my masculine/assertive qualities and let go of my fear, anxieties and the over-developed, emotionally complex side of my nature.

FEBRUARY 1998

Titanic

Days later – as serendipity would have it – I went to the cinema with my then husband, to see the film *Titanic*, starring Kate Winslet and Leonardo Dicaprio. The date was February 4th 1998, and the film had just been released in the UK. At this point (because I could barely walk without suffering immense pain and being in bed for days afterwards) I had to use a wheelchair; at thirty-two, this was not something that I did often – I tended to stay at home rather than go out in it – as I hated it so much.

As you will know, *Titanic* is a love story between the two main characters with the backdrop of the real life tragedy of the unsinkable ship, which did in fact sink, with great loss of life. In the story, their intense and short-lived love affair is relived by an ageing Rose, as she remembers the experience and the loss of Jack before being saved herself! A true damsel in distress who overcomes her fate!

Along with the internal work I was doing and, due to the fact I had completely surrendered to the divine in 1997 after reading *A Return to Love*, I was very open to change and willing to do whatever I had to do to be well and to heal!

Titanic for me symbolised my own love story that had 'gone wrong' many years previously, and which seemed to be irresolvable to me. Perhaps it was another cathartic moment, as I just cried for next couple of days. As Jack Kornfield says in his book *A Path With Heart* until we have cried deeply a number of times there can be no real release and spiritual healing. Certainly I had cried before but there are different types of tears – these were tears of grief – unresolved, untouchable grief that I had kept so well buried and inaccessible that I had been unable to feel it fully and had been numb!

Jack Engler, a Buddhist teacher and psychologist at Harvard University, has described meditation practice as primarily a practice of grieving and letting go. At most spiritual retreats, nearly half of the students are working with some level of grief, denial, anger, loss or sorrow. Out of this work comes a deep renewal.

My entry in my spiritual diary for 5/2/98, was recorded after watching *Titanic* and feeling the mixed emotions I had been plagued by for nearly ten years. While in Corfu in July 1988, I had a mystical experience, and while I was there, I happened to fall in love. This really opened my life to my own hero's journey, just as *Titanic* is the story of a damsel in distress. Rose (played by Kate Winslet) – was being married off to a rich man she neither loved nor wanted – so my own damsel felt abandoned by God, leaving me feeling lonely and uncertain of my fate at this time.

5/2/98

A wish

The passion and intensity of a stolen kiss
Rise up in me and make me wish
For a reckless, wild lost weekend
When everything else pales into insignificance
And helps me forget

The pain, loss and despair I experience every day when I stir
To feast on forbidden fruit
And pretend my fantasy and dream
Is real and pure and true
Exquisite like a fresh flower
Or bright like the golden sun
Shining down on me as I run
To a new life of joy and fun!
But then I jolt back to today
And I remember the sweet sacrifice
And selfless love I am surrounded by
And I know I can be renewed
And feel alive and look ahead
With joy
If only this great chain would snap and release
Me into a new day with Sandy
Of light and air and let go of all cares!

I had the realisation that day, that I needed to let go – really let go – and in that moment. I went back to my wedding day – a day when I had committed to closing the chapter on Corfu where I had fallen in love with Michael – and start afresh as a married woman with a new name and follow my calling as best I could!

I was married on 8th September 1989, and a few months after the wedding it was decided that my new husband and I would start a new life together, working with VSO as volunteers in an aid project. We would leave in the January; we were excited about doing this and felt that it was an important step in our life together. Service to others seemed natural and uplifting for us both, and the Minister had commended our decision publicly at our wedding, which felt to me like this was God's will for my life.

I completed my sick children's training at Yorkhill Hospital in Glasgow, and then waited in anticipation for a date and destination. I wanted to go as far away as possible from my old life and make a fresh start, hoping this would bring me true joy.

So I continued to study astrology in search of answers and did some nurse agency work to help with paying the bills while we waited for our placement.

However, fatigue set in and, like the previous year, I wondered what was the matter with me! My mood swings were worse and it felt like I was constantly tired and tense. I was not easy to live with; wishing Sandy would turn into Michael and all would be well, I lapsed between my new fantasy world and the reality that no longer held my attention.

My confidence seemed low; I clung to Sandy more than ever and yet I feared this emotional dependence. I would storm out of the flat after our frequent arguments and berate God for dealing me this hand. However, I quickly decided that I needed to learn something from Sandy, accept that I was married, and in doing so, Michael would appear again one day and make things better. Yes, this was a crazy thought, but feeling as if I was disintegrating from inside, I began to sense that my health was on a downward slide.

By late spring of 1990, I became ill with flu. At that time I was offered an interview at the local homeopathic hospital; the hot weather did little to warm me, and therefore I wrapped myself up in order to aid me in my recovery.

I was successful at the interview and offered a 22.5 hours contract. I was over the moon. I loved living in the fashionable west end of Glasgow and, as VSO hadn't come up with any placements yet, I felt we should settle down and enjoy what we had!

Due to the ongoing range of odd symptoms I had, I began to delve into complementary healing methods looking for relief from the tension, muscle twitchings, night sweats and general moodiness, which I now seemed to get on a regular basis. I began reading self-help nutritional health books to try to make sense of it all and sought advice from a wide range of complementary therapists that I felt could support my healing.

My husband Sandy was not so pleased about the job. His dream was to go abroad, whether it was with VSO or not. We explored other options;

Canada and Australia. I was accepted; however, he was rejected due to his medication for his asthma.

Finally, in June 1990, we received a call from VSO London. The senior placement officer informed us that our destination was to be Nepal. It was situated next to the Indian border and around 200 miles south of Kathmandu. We would work on a nursing campus, teaching student nurses basic nursing care.

Having always wanted to go to Nepal it sounded like it was a great way to experience a new culture, be of service, escape from my past, and reconcile myself with my decision to marry! It would take another three years before I was eventually diagnosed with ME, and really face what was to become my own biggest challenge to heal my life and body from this chronic and severe condition by becoming more aware of my own life purpose!

New Beginnings

FEBRUARY 1998

After the release of emotions through watching *Titanic* and being inspired by Celine Dion's moving song *My heart will go on,* I wrote *New Beginnings* as I really wanted my life to change and was willing to take the necessary action to back it up!

This is what I wrote to affirm this new belief.

6/2/98

Today is a new day I want to see life in a new way
Freed from the fear and pain and despair
I often seem to wear
To cast off the old
And start to feel more bold
And daring and free
And set adrift from past habits
Past loss and past despair and beyond care
I try to think in a new way
Of hope and joy and love

Because I too can enjoy
The fruits and jewels of this sweet world
Instead of always seeing it reflected
In others' eyes and turning away
Believing that it's not for me
So today is that day
When I divide the present from the past
And make the effort
To start to believe wholly in me!
Illuminated with new wisdom
And having learnt the lessons
Of days gone past
I start today as I want to go on
With determination and courage and the plan
Of new vitality, energy and hope
And the knowledge that I can!

As much as I was moving forward at this time and making new choices, my body continued to be beyond healing and I wrote *Battlefield* on 7th February 1998, because that is how my life felt. My body was that battlefield and the conflict that raged within it was the illness. I truly dislike labels – all labels. They create separation, pain and unnecessary suffering in my opinion. Therefore, my take on the malady that was in full control of my life was something I saw more as a message from God in relation to changing me. I was not too keen on how it was changing me nor could I see much light at the end of the proverbial tunnel! Despite my hope from the previous day's entry *New Beginnings* it was back to business as usual, and healing felt like a two-step forwards and one-step back dance.

As I studied astrology (and had been doing astrology readings for paying clients for quite a few years) I felt I was somehow above the label of specific illness. Yes, I had to write it in medical forms; however, I had given up on support groups and all the whingeing that often goes along with them.

I knew deep inside why this was happening to me; from my astrology chart, the experiences that I had endured as a child, and from the books and information that were being steadily sent in my direction (which I read ravenously like a starving child at a feast). My life was about healing family Karma and being the receptacle for the transformation through that healing – but still the pieces of my jigsaw eluded me!

7/2/98

Battlefield

My body is a battlefield
The right fights with the left for supremacy
Leaving me torn in two
And screaming with frustration
As I stagger along
Muscles twitching, heart beating like fire
And my brain convulsing
As it tries to right this sinking ship
I lick my wounds in between
Moments of respite when I click in
But they are fleeting
Only allowing me to draw breath
Before the next offensive
I walk blind unknowing where
Or when the next attack will surface
Fear intermingled with relief
As I swing from one extreme to another
Losing control, lashing me down
Spinning like a whirlpool
Of symptoms, emotions and despair
As I try in vain to take the reins
Of my life and steer the path
Of middle ground, safety and peace.
I weep silent tears
For all the lost years
I have fought my fears
Of disability, insanity and anxiety
Tense, and ready for the next attack.

I had read *The Alchemy of Illness* in 1995. It is a fantastic book by Kat Duff, all about how when we remove our illness from the realm of strictly personal, and then place it in the larger context of social realities and spiritual laws, all kinds of light bulbs start to glow in the darkness. I highly recommend it for anyone who is struck by a chronic condition and is looking for fresh insights and some much-needed understanding of yourself, and away from the judgements of others!

My way of giving myself a break was to lock myself away and read some enlightening literature – 'soul food' as my future 'guru' Caroline Myss would say (we hadn't met at this point -in fact I didn't know of the delights that lay ahead of me that would unfold once we were to be connected by the Divine) and have a cup of tea while I made some sense of the jigsaw puzzle of my life. More order was sought and the books that winged their way to me were and still are some of my most treasured possessions.

Kat had Chronic Fatigue syndrome and a great deal of conscious awareness, too, if the book and healing quest it takes you on are anything to go by. I gleaned from it that she had been sexually abused as a child and that this was somehow connected with her descent into the lower worlds. I knew this place only too well.

Having Pluto in my 12th house of my own birth chart and, being on intimate terms with Persephone, I had spent most of the last few winters in her domain – flat on my back!

Usually I would go into remission in the spring and relapse in the late autumn and winter – yes, I was a living, breathing example of the myth. I was also pretty well acquainted with Ereshkigal (from the Inannna myth) and how one is stripped of everything to serve a higher purpose. So all of this was fascinating stuff and I knew it intellectually; however, I wasn't truly feeling it and so the journalling and dark night of the soul journey were to be my greatest achievements in healing all the garbage that I had chosen to work with in this incarnation! You see; the gold is in there – it is just deeply hidden – your very own treasure chest. Another symbol of Pluto is the buried treasure within your unconscious. After Hercules has raised the Hydra and cut off all nine of her heads, a tenth one appears, which is a jewel. The monster yields something precious in the end.

As the poet Rilke states:

> *"Perhaps all the dragons of our lives are princesses who are only*
> *waiting to see us once beautiful and brave.*
> *Perhaps everything terrible is in its deepest being something*
> *helpless that wants help from us."*

So insights from my soul were taking me on a journey deeply into my unconscious and showing me that all that had happened in my life was serving a greater purpose (my Sacred Purpose), but if only I could co-operate and stop fighting it.

> *"Consciously lived suffering has a redeeming effect upon the*
> *past and future of mankind, an effect which is exerted invisibly*
> *from the beyond"* Marie-Louise Von Franz

I continued to work with the book on *Being Your Own Counsellor* and this brought me to explore my family history. I knew at a deep level that much of my personal suffering was connected to my family history and that the romance I had had in Corfu in 1988 with Michael was connected to my Gran's past. I had even had a dream in 1991 whilst in Nepal doing VSO that seemed to confirm this.

In the dream, I was 'told' that the reason I was ill was that my Mum did not know who her real father was. It happened the same day as I received a letter from my friend Anne, who had been in Corfu with me, and she described how she had just been to Belfast for a visit but had not seen Michael at Marks & Spencer, where he had told us he busked for extra money. It was a joke of course on her part, but to say I felt haunted by it all was an understatement!

Root Chakra and family History

Understanding how we are all one!

FEBRUARY 1941

Ivy straightened her hair and applied a little more rouge to her pale cheeks.

Picking up her handbag, she closed the door firmly behind her and felt the excitement start to fill her small, lithe frame. She was meeting Joe again – perhaps for the last time. His ship would sail out from Clydebank tonight and she had no idea when she might see him again. The singing from the nearby pub and some drunken soldiers met her as she walked to their usual meeting place.

NOVEMBER 1941

The baby cried taking her first breath and felt two strong hands wipe her clean and wrap her tightly in the warm cosy blanket. Ivy Ness gazed at the child half in fear and half in adoration: "Maureen. I will name her Maureen!"

My Mum was born illegitimate in 1941. Maureen Hamilton Ness. Her mother chose to keep her despite all the problems that this involved. Somehow too attached to this new baby and unable to let her go, she prayed she would cope. Perhaps Joe would come back. Perhaps his ship had gone down in the war. She did not know but needed to find out!

The carers at the maternity home and in the church promised to help her find him. He would marry her surely and all would be well. This shame would be released and forgotten. With so many other things going on in wartime, she felt sure that people would forget and she could have all that she dreamed of. So she waited in hope and prayed that she would cope until he came back.

Two years later she got married – but it was not to Joe. His name was Alexander Kelly (sometimes called Sandy) and he was a good man. He loved Maureen. In fact, he had fallen for her, which was how he got talking to Ivy. Shy and somewhat brusque around women, he felt able to talk to the bairn and she responded. This had brought Ivy out of her shell and they decided to be married.

He would adopt Maureen and they would have children of their own – their own little family unit – safe and sound.

Here is my Mum's story in her own words

"I was born in Rottenrow Hospital in Glasgow on 11th November 1941 to Sarah Ivy Moir Ness. I was illegitimate and in 1941 (although there were many people in the same position) that was a stigma, which stayed with me for many years. Of course, I did not realise as a baby or as a child, until I was school age that I was carrying a label. My mother had been in private service in the north-east of Scotland, but had given up her work in 1939 to care for her dying mother. After Granny's death and, with the coming of war, she went to work in a munitions factory as part of the war effort. During that time, she became pregnant, lost her job, her digs, and was left more or less destitute. Nobody wanted to know her and she was too ashamed to go home and tell her father. She went to Glasgow and was found there by a Glasgow policeman, wandering about, as she did not know the city. He noted her condition and took her to a Church of Scotland home for unmarried mothers in the west end of Glasgow near Woodside Church. She stayed there until after I was born, and then after my birth, they found my mother a job as housekeeper at Orchard House in the Clyde Valley, which was owned by R & W Scott Jam Makers. I was very fortunate in that the people who lived in Orchard House were all very good to me and we stayed there until Mum married Alex Kelly on 29th April 1944. Once married, she and the man who became my Dad moved to Orchard Lodge and my earliest memory is of moving to that little lodge to stay.

When I went to school, I was a bright spark – always top of the class, which I enjoyed as I hated to be beaten and especially as the Scott family always rewarded me with five shillings every time I won an award or a prize. By this time, I was the richest member of the family as I had over £30 in the bank – a fortune in those days – all given to me by the Scott family for my education in later life. However, one day I was coming home from school with Archie Waddell, who was in the same class as me. There had been a test that day and I had beaten Archie into second place once again, so I was feeling quite pleased with myself. As we neared home, we met Archie's mother, who asked him how he got on in the test. He told her he was second and I was first and she turned to me and gave me a telling off saying that it was a disgrace that her son had to go to school to be beaten by a bastard. I went home, asked my mother what a bastard was, and related the conversation with Mrs Waddell. Unfortunately all hell was let loose and I felt very guilty at having caused a problem, although I didn't know what the problem was."

And so it appeared to be my fate to have been incarnated in this lifetime to heal family Karma and follow a path of resolving it for myself and my ancestors. I turned to astrology for answers and discovered it was linked to my full 12th house in my birth chart (ruled by Neptune traditionally) and that the feelings of having to surrender to something greater than myself were guiding me. Transcendence was just a word; however, I knew somehow that I had to get there and reach my own enlightenment to be free of it all and live my destiny!

RESOURCES AND EXERCISES FOR CHAPTER 1

Neptune – your innermost light

Neptune is the planet, which rules Pisces and the 12th house of the zodiac. It is related to **The Victim, The Poet** and **The Mystic**. I include it here as it shows how we swim through Neptunian waters as a victim until we can transcend and reach the realisation that we can become the director and creator of our destiny rather than a pawn!

Neptune is the ruler of Pisces and the 12th house in astrology

Neptune is the planet of illusion and dreams, and tends to spiritualise our lives in a big way. It is associated with divine discontent and puts us in touch with our urge for perfection, the sublime and enlightenment. It often causes us to feel disillusioned as a means of leading us out of our self-imposed prison of illusion and thus putting us in touch with our own inspiration and spirituality. It is often prominent at times of peak experiences; or when we fall in love, and helps us to be reunited with the source and unconditional love for all life. It encourages us to merge with something greater than ourselves and dissolves boundaries in our lives. It is associated with art, music and all forms of creative self-expression, which help us to be in the moment and express love. It spends fourteen years in each sign of the zodiac and takes 165 years to complete one revolution of our chart. It moved into the sign of Pisces in February 2012 and will be there for approximately fourteen years. Resolution is happening for so many people with this shift!

Eleven key states to enlightenment*

a. **The Foggy State** – This is when you feel half awake/half asleep. You may space out easily in this stage or feel like you need a strong caffeinated drink to wake you up as you easily forget names, dates and

---

*Adapted from *The astrology of Self Discovery* by Tracy Marks

lose track of time. Not usually a pleasant state though, some Pisceans/ Neptunian types live here for long periods of time and manage OK! Confusion reigns here and you may feel like there is no clear direction for long spells when you are undergoing a transformation by Neptune. Therefore, this becomes a familiar state, especially when Neptune is close to a personal planet in your chart for the first time. You can feel like someone has drugged you. The upside is that confusion can be a very high state and allows you to explore the unknown and attract options you may have ignored or refused to see before!

a. **The Intersection State** – You may still feel half asleep in this state but there is more clarity of perception. It is similar to the pre-and post-sleep state, where you may get insights or dream images just as you fall asleep (Hypnagogic) or wake up (Hypnopompic). It is the intersection of the two worlds – inner and outer.

a. **The Fantasy State** – This is the dreamy state where you enjoy little daydreams and may lose awareness of yourself for periods. It can be a very receptive state, which you do not always control – just enjoying what is flowing through you and allowing it to occur and unfold. At other times, you may direct it towards a fantasy or visualisation, but this is likely to be occurring with minimal conscious effort.

a. **The Dream State** – In this state, you have no self-awareness or consciousness as you are asleep. Themes which occur repeatedly in your dreams, may be linked to Neptune (in your birth chart or by transit) and your 12th house as higher forms of guidance.

a. **The Meditative State** – Deep relaxation or Alpha state occurs, where awareness is focussed inwards, while observing the inner processes. Perception is clear here.

a. **The Psychic State** – You may or may not be focussed on your internal experiences but are highly receptive to images and impressions. You easily tune into guidance here.

a. **The Highly Focussed Inner State** – This is where you know you are being guided by your higher self – you may receive images and be clairaudient/claircognizant in this –state – so be advised to record insights and guidance for future reference.

a. **The Artificial State** – This state is often induced by drugs or alcohol. Negative energy and repressed material can be released in this state, such as when taking LSD or when very drunk and this can translate into hallucinations or cause you to feel out of control (mental illness is linked to this state).

a. **The Creative Inspiration State** – An outwardly focussed state; awareness is heightened and visionary states can occur here, leading to a trance-like state of transformation and change.

a. **The Opening Your Heart State** – In which the pains and sensitivities of the past may wash over you. You may feel considerable love and compassion for others here. You begin to transcend your own desires and love from the divine source within you.

a. **Enlightenment State** – The 11th and final state is where mystical experiences or cosmic consciousness takes over and your boundaries completely drop, as your ego merges with spirit and you receive an influx of healing and rejuvenating cosmic energy.

Enlightenment – This is the state referred to as 'enlightenment', as we see we are the Universe and have complete knowing of everything. This rarely lasts for more than a few hours; it is usually called a peak experience that can catapult you into a new spiritual consciousness e.g. NDE and Kundalini Awakening etc.

You may find that you fluctuate in one or two states more frequently than others mentioned here. We all have the ability to access each state and we may experience the first nine states on a regular basis if we are on a spiritual path. States ten and eleven occur less frequently and usually only last for brief periods of time. You can tap into Neptune, which is a watery planet to help you swim through these states and tune into where you are at on this scale to assist you to move up a level.

Each state has a gift for you. For example, being in the fog can help you learn new ways of navigating rather than simply depending on your vision

– your senses are heightened, you slow down, smell the roses and hear the crickets – so it is with these psychic states. You may tune into parts of yourself that you never knew existed under a prominent Neptune transit and emerge with a new perspective as you dissolve the old you into a wiser and more mature YOU.

Neptune helps you to move through victim consciousness into oneness, consciousness and unification with all life!

The Victim Archetype
Moving from Victim to Warrior

The story of the Wizard of Oz is a masterpiece at conveying the higher truths of the four Universal Archetypes within a Sacred Contract.

This is exactly what this film depicts – the journey of each of the four – into continuity. What we've got in the Sovereign, is the journey of the child (see chapter 4, Dorothy) to have authority over herself, to be able to maintain balance, to listen to her team in the shape of the Tin Man, the Lion and the Scarecrow for advice, but not be dictated to by them). This is the wise counsel for the Sovereign. These four Archetypes work like a chorus and the helpers encourage her to take the lead and to do what is empowering for self AND the three others she subsequently meets on the way to find the wonderful Wizard of Oz! They find a 'common purpose' to get to Oz, get help for their shortcomings and through wisdom, work from that stance to gain the highest prize of all – true spiritual identity and fulfilment of your Sacred Contracts by coming together for the common good. This is a mystical truth: "What is in one is in the whole." What is good for you should be good for all, and vice versa!

One of the four Universal Archetypes is The Victim. It is Universal because we all have to navigate this one!

Victim Archetype: Your Guardian of self-esteem is transformed into your Warrior once you are empowered and living your destiny!

You want your own Warrior that is, your General, to go forward with courage. Your Warrior takes the action and advises on what helps you to actualise your goals and purpose in this life. The Warrior is a very noble Archetype almost like the protector of your boundaries. It is the one that takes action to protect, so that you can say "Yes" when you mean yes, and "No" when you mean no; so that you're not manipulated by everybody else's needs, so that you're not victimized and there's nothing left of you! The Warrior knows where to set the boundary and say: "STOP, that's enough – no more! You can try me anyway you want, and you don't cross this line." The Victim cannot do that. The Victim does not have the power to protect that.

Here are some questions to ask yourself, related to The Victim Archetype – often symbolised by Neptune in your birth chart.

Step into your Victim and ask yourself the following questions:

1. When you look at the world through the eyes of your Victim what are your main problems?

2. What are you telling yourself?

3. Who or what are you blaming?

4. When you feel victimised by others, what has happened?

5. What is your life lesson around playing the Victim?

6. How can you get back to a place of empowerment?

7. Who do you need to forgive or release to move forward?

8. How have you transformed your Victim into your Warrior in the past?

9. What particular wisdom have you learnt from your Victim Archetype so that you never victimise others in that way again?

Chapter 2

THE KEYS TO UNLOCK YOUR TREASURE

"You must be the change you want to see in the world." – Gandhi

I was fascinated by astrology from a young age. Nothing and no one encouraged it in my family! It just resonated so strongly inside that I knew that one day I had to look into it. I had no idea how one became an astrologer but due to a series of serendipitous events I did indeed study it at classes in Glasgow in 1988. That was the year that my life changed; I knew and experienced the mystery that became the source of my 'itch'. Something BIG woke up then and led me on this intense path of self-discovery.

I had actually purchased my first book that took me into 'real astrology' called *Cast Your Own Horoscope* in December 1986. I completed my nurses' training that year and moved to a small town called Falkirk in central Scotland to take on my first post as a staff nurse. I was 21 years old and it felt like a big responsibility to be in charge of a ward. I was also feeling quite isolated as my nurse friends had all gone their separate ways to new jobs or had married and settled down to have children. I still had my boyfriend of two years, Sandy, who I saw quite frequently but he lived some 30 miles away and worked shifts as a nurse too. So at the time I was feeling quite lonely and was starting to seek out new answers and get to know myself a bit better. As I no longer had my friends close by or other distractions around me, I was at a bit of a loose end one day!

I remember walking into WH Smith one frosty December afternoon in 1986 and seeing this astrology book called *Cast Your Own Horoscope*. I bought it and took it home to explore further. In casting my own horoscope I discovered that my rising sign or ascendant as it is called, was in the airy sign of Libra and that there were twelve houses or sectors of life. So this was to be the first key that would unlock the treasures within me. It was a bit like a taster session and whetted my appetite for more – much more!

I would later discover through my soul-centred astrology teacher and friend Gary Kidgell, that the key words for my soul's purpose (at age 21) were being acted out in that moment namely: *"I've got the key of the door, i.e. astrology, psychology, physiology."*

At that point, in December 1986, I was simply following my guidance and beginning to unravel the mystery of my life and purpose to help me to cope with what was a difficult time.

Between December 1986 and May 1988, I worked as a staff nurse. I started working at a Geriatric ward caring for elderly people and then moved onto a medical and surgical ward – spending six months in each posting. I also acquired a cat called Tigger and bought my first flat. So I was trying to be responsible and live my life as best as I could. I bought a bike, cycled to work every day, and took more exercise than ever before! I was trying to stop smoking completely and was no longer using alcohol as an escape mechanism. So I was maturing and trying to become a 'better person'. For me, astrology seemed to shine a light on some of my harmful 'addictions' and I read this first book with great interest. I did well at work and by the end of my eighteen months there, I had been promoted to the post of Senior Staff Nurse (Grade E).

I still felt unhappy though, as if something was missing and I could not quite put my finger on it. I also wanted to get married and have children.

To me life could be simple and straightforward. My boyfriend Sandy was not so keen to settle down although we were quite happy together and had been dating for over three years. I felt like I was searching for something more. Astrology was the key that would open Aladdin's cave for me and I wanted to learn more!

In studying astrology I discovered that horoscope literally means the *hour* as in *horo* and scope means the range of abilities we are born with. So in effect, it means you were born at a certain hour with the talent or ability attributable to the planetary arrangement and to some extent, this is set at your birth. Your birth chart indicates your 'fate' or as Carl Jung said, "Character is fate" and the birth chart is a blueprint that maps out who you are and how you are likely to interact in the Universe.

I would also later discover that there are seven-year cycles and I had started a new one at age 21. It's almost like being programmed to take a new initiation every seven years and astrology was to be part of my path, and my guide from there on. A different sign rules each seven-year cycle, so between 21 and 28, I was in the Cancer cycle, which is related to home, family and inheritance! It was little wonder then that I was being furnished with answers regarding my own inherited Karma from my ancestors, and given the means to heal myself through studying astrology and my own soul's purpose.

Twelve months after buying *Cast Your Own Horoscope,* I read a very insightful article all about Saturn and how it impacts us. Saturn is the cosmic schoolteacher and helps us to stay grounded and learn whatever lessons we have agreed to in this lifetime! It was in the sign of Sagittarius between 1986 and 1989 (it actually spends 2.5 years in each sign) and being a sun sign Sagittarian, 1987–88 had been a time of intense grounded learning all about me!

That period was like a huge watershed in my life. Astrology became the guide, illuminated my path with new insights, and gave me the fortitude to walk my path. When I read some of my favourite spiritual teachers echoing that back to me years later, I was vindicated!

In *Why People Don't Heal and How They Can,* Caroline Myss states: "For reasons I may never understand 1988 was the year when views and beliefs about healing shifted."

Errol Weiner states in *Transpersonal Astrology: Finding the Soul's Purpose:* "The years 1988–90 were profound in terms of human evolution."

1987–88 was a rude awakening in many ways but one I had been praying for; I knew I really could not keep living life the way I had been before. Too much alcohol, emotional repression and fears about myself had left me and my ego feeling pretty fragile.

I had tried hypnosis and yoga to get to the bottom of it all and heal these issues but nothing really seemed to work! In fact, the hypnotherapist I had seen had been more focussed on seducing me. Not a laughing matter and this had put me off seeing anymore therapists for a while. I made my escape from him and breathed a sigh of relief!

In February of that year, I visited the astrology centre based at St Stephen's Street in Edinburgh. It was featured on a programme I had seen on TV all about astrology. So I took the train over there to discover more with my boyfriend.

I bought my first computerised astrology chart, which was based on my date, time and place of birth and another book called *Teach Yourself Astrology* by Jeff Mayo that day. I also discovered there were classes and a group I could attend in Glasgow at The Theosophical Society. In many ways that partly shaped my decision to leave Falkirk, and then move to Glasgow to train as a sick children's nurse a few months later.

I started facing what I had been unable to prior to 1988 and so began my journey of self-discovery. A solar eclipse triggered off my soul's purpose that year and I woke up to something greater than I felt able to deal with. Astrology would show me the way and help me to unlock my treasures!

Astrology is thus an important key and one I recommend as getting you started on your own journey to healing and empowerment. (See diagram 1 in resources and recommendations.)

Key 2

Dream work and journalling

I have worked with my dreams consciously since 1990. I bought the book *Your Secret Self -illuminating the mysteries of the 12th House* by Tracy Marks in May 1990. Almost immediately, my dreams started to come fast and furious!

This dream on 1/6/90 was a precursor for my illness becoming more 'visible' and in hindsight was an indication of what lay ahead.

I dream that my face is disfigured on the right side. My sister is by me and cuddling me to help me feel better. I do not feel I am disfigured and I am just glad to be accepted for the way I look. I am looking forward to my face healing and I am crying a lot! Other people around me are distressed by my emotions but I do not feel weak or hopeless.

Using astrology and my new knowledge, I followed my dreams for guidance and insights to help me to heal. In 1994 when I was physically at my lowest ebb, they gave me hope that I would recover. At that point, I was pretty much flat out on the couch and was on the highest level of antidepressants. I kept dreaming that I would recover. Something within me refused to give up hope and my dreams supported me in the belief that a miracle was possible. I started reading stories about people in dreadfully difficult situations to give me hope. The hostages in Beirut were being released at this time and I read *Some Other Rainbow* by John McCarthy and Jill Morrell. I also read *In the Name of the Father* by Gerry Conlon of The Guildford Four and *Alive* based on the book about the rugby team stranded on a mountain. All these books and films gave me hope that I could miraculously heal, which filtered into my dreams. In reality, my life seemed bleak and I felt like no one believed in me or cared. This probably was not true but it was how I felt!

I withdrew into my world of the soul, sensing the answer lay within me. I felt sure that somehow I could get well and heal whatever this dreadful condition was bringing to my attention. Although it seemed unhealable at that time, my inner strength and spirit kept me alive through my dreams, astrology, and the belief that there was a reason or purpose behind it all!

Key 3

Archetypes and Casting Your Sacred Contract

The third and final key to really understanding my life purpose happened some twenty years later. It was December 2008 and I had come full circle, and was again in a 'stuck' place. In many ways astrology, dreamwork, journalling and coaching, had unlocked much of my life purpose. I just knew that something else was required! That is when I moved onto the final BIG key.

Casting your Sacred Contract is like that. It is an intention and by activating it, suddenly everything starts to ignite and the dormant forces that were sleeping wake up!

It all started at New Year in 2009 for me, though I had inklings of unrest throughout 2008. I have always known that my life purpose was much bigger than the little me that I have put out there – you are probably the same! As I have explained, I was born into an unusual family with enough skeletons and ghosts from the past to require something miraculous to heal it! Moreover, I knew from analysing my birth chart that it was my fate to be the catalyst to heal the family Karma.

You see, your Sacred Contract is a mystery that has been with you all your life at the deeply unconscious level. It's that itch that you want to scratch and can never fully get to... until you do!

So when I look back at my whole life it is no surprise to me at all that I ended up attracting Caroline Myss and her work into my life!

All the fears and excuses that I gave myself for why my life couldn't possibly be the way I knew I wanted it to be suddenly evaporated.

By working through the process that Sacred Contracts is and feeling the higher vibratory energy it releases into you at the level of personality, I suddenly moved from being an observer to being the main character in my life plan and purpose. Something big changed internally and with it, my external world started throwing out things that had been dormant and unexplained for nearly twenty years!

So what is your Sacred Contract?

An agreement you have made with the divine prior to your birth to experience, certain key events, relationships, challenges and opportunities that will script your personal life plan and enable you to fulfil your mission or sacred purpose in this lifetime. This life plan is your Sacred Contract!

You have been given a support team of twelve Archetypes that will be your teachers as you play this out in reality. These Archetypes as identified by Carl Jung are Universal patterns of power and can be seen as your life essence and contain the talents and attributes that make you uniquely YOU!

The aim of connecting with your Sacred Contract is to: *move past the contract your ego would like you to have to the contract your soul actually agreed to.*

To really connect and activate this contract requires two questions:

Where am I going?

Who will go with me?

An understanding of the *bigger picture and* knowing yourself will help you to respond appropriately and align with your contract allowing everything you require to enable it to unfold just as it should.

The divine ultimately is asking for your total trust and surrender to what you agreed to when in spirit form. Remember you agreed to this life plan and it is all there waiting for you. In doing this you align with divine will, which is the highest form of service and the greatest struggle for your ego, which is to let go and let God. This is what is required to fulfil your Sacred Contracts and understand what you were born to do!

"Every contract holds that hidden jewel, that hidden doorway that leads you deeper into yourself. People are often too focused on 'the other', not understanding that the person opposite them is a catalyst, not an object to be owned, dominated or controlled. If a person can

truly grasp that, they find their way to what is sacred within them-selves and 'the other', as they no longer make the object of a relation-ship control. All roads ultimately lead to the sacred." – Caroline Myss

One example of this (because there are too many to mention) was that my grandmother (aged 95) passed on the day I left for Chicago. She had been ill and in hospital with a stroke for six weeks and, having already made it to Belfast at the start of May 2009 and meeting the woman who has since become my mentor, I knew it was no accident!

You see, I met someone from Belfast in July 1988; that changed my life, and who I told my whole life story to! He was probably as gobsmacked as me when I did but it was like a release of everything I had kept bottled up for years. Once I told him, I had what can only be described as a mystical experience that was way out of my understanding, but which opened my heart to something much much larger than I could ever have envisaged.

And a lot of this was to do with my Grandmother (my mother's mother).

As I have explained in chapter one, my Mum was born on 11th of November in the war – a chaotic period when many lives changed. My Mum never knew her real father or what became of him, and it was a big secret in my family – and this was part of the mystery of my own life!

So when my Gran had a stroke on Maundy Thursday I knew this was a pivotal moment in my own life. As synchronicity would have it, Susan Boyle would become famous within a few days of this with her appearance on Britain's Got Talent. She sang *I Dreamed a Dream* from Les Miserables and opened the hearts of millions of cynical people around the globe. Coming from Scotland myself and, feeling that my own life was somehow passing me by, it held some significance for me too!

Six weeks later, my Gran passed on, the very day I left for Chicago to study Sacred Contracts with Caroline Myss, I knew it was significant.

Little did I know that I was about to meet someone famous as I flew to Chicago via London.

It was Jim Kerr of the pop band Simple Minds and he was two rows in front of me on the plane. At first I tried to ignore him, as I wasn't even sure it was him and then I just knew I had to check or I would always believe I had imagined it!

Therefore, running up behind him after we got off the plane, he suddenly stopped to make a call and that was my moment. So I asked him: "Are you Jim Kerr?" and he said, "Yes!" and "Here's Charlie Burchill," also of the band Simple Minds!

I blurted out, "My goodness! YOU are part of my Sacred Contract!" to which he asked: "What is that?" I said, "Well, it's our life plan that we agreed to before we were born to activate and live our soul's purpose in this lifetime. And today I am going to Chicago and my Grandmother who had been a very significant player in it has just passed on." Plus, I had just returned from Belfast where another key player in it lives.

So I got his autograph and my picture taken with him and I explained that the contract related to his song *Don't You Forget About Me*. The guy I met on holiday had written it in my diary 21 years previously with a drawing of himself and the band's name above it! How could I ever have known that 21 years later this mystery was a big step nearer making sense! So, my next question was: "Is this my fate or is it my destiny?"

I did not know for sure at that moment but I did know that my life was undergoing a radical shift. Having cast my own Sacred Contract in March of 2009 with my Damsel Archetype landing at the very top (in the highest potential house) it all suddenly began to make much more sense! (See diagram 2)

I had met my millionaire mentor Bernadette Doyle in Belfast three weeks earlier and something told me that my old life as a nurse was coming to its end!

So you may ask what's all this about and how can it help to understand your Sacred Contract.

An Archetype is a Universal pattern of power and we each have our very own team of twelve assisting us to know and fulfil the life path and purpose we chose to incarnate into and fulfil.

> *Archetypes are your energy guides to your highest potential –*
> *the fulfilment of your Sacred contract C Myss.*

So by understanding the light and shadow of each member of your team and the area that they hold court, in your Sacred Contract this divining tool shines the light on each of them and brings what has been unconscious to greater conscious awareness!

By casting my contract and gaining new insights, it really put me back into the driving seat of my life.

The dynamic of the Damsel in her light and shadow qualities, and the counterpart she often attracts in the Knight (no pun intended here!) had greatly shaped my life path. Given my family history, I felt an instant 'aha!' when I had cast it and the Damsel came out at the top of my chart!

So first of all what is the Damsel Archetype all about?

A damsel is always beautiful, vulnerable and in need of rescue specifically by a knight. Once she is rescued, she wants to be taken care of in lavish style in a palace. For some damsels this may turn into a castle and be more akin to a prison than a life of luxury! When disappointed, the lesson for the damsel is to become empowered and to learn to take care of herself (hence the well-known term damsel in distress). Once the damsel takes on the spiritual quest for empowerment, she learns skills and competencies and how to take good care of herself without the necessity of rescue by the knight! The area the Damsel shows up in your life is indicative of your struggle with the Archetype and how this can be the training ground for transformation and personal empowerment!

Many women may at the deeply unconscious level be damsels; however, in a time of female emancipation and liberation, she may indeed still want a knight, but not specifically to save her. She may want a knight just to hold her hand as she walks her own path and with whom she can be vulnerable in a romantic way, as she shares her spiritual path with him as her mate! That is what I call spiritual transformation and being able to own your Archetypal energies without fear!

For me, I had certainly played out this damsel in distress and I could see quite clearly that this pattern had been passed down my family line. My Gran had been abandoned and ended up having my Mum on her own. She had subsequently married but this 'wound' left its mark on her and years later history would repeat itself and my Aunt had suffered a similar 'fate'. My turn came as I sensed it would (as a child) in 1988 in Corfu and ultimately healing this wound was part of my purpose! Until I truly gave up the notion that anyone was coming to rescue me, I simply repeated this pattern, experienced a lot of psychic, and inherited pain through it – my own and that of my family!

And what of the Knight?

Well, the knight is associated with chivalry and courtly romance. He will protect the damsel and be willing to undergo self-sacrifice because of loyalty. This is fine if he is with the damsel he has a Sacred Contract with! The shadow side of the Knight is the absence of honour and chivalry. Specifically he may be loyal to a questionable principle or Damsel and indeed may be sacrificing his own needs, purpose and highest potential by remaining the rescuer in a relationship that no longer fulfils his contract! A true Knight has a pattern of service to others and, like the mystic, walks a fine line between self-sacrifice and self-neglect.

The Knight may have to be willing to separate himself from inappropriate damsels and honour his own spiritual path, whilst trusting that there may be other damsels out there that can walk the spiritual path with him too!

Diagram 1 – My birth chart
Natal for Gill Potter

15 December 1965 Time: 01:35:00 Zone: 00:00:00

East Kilbride Lat: 55:46:00 N Long: 004:11:00 W

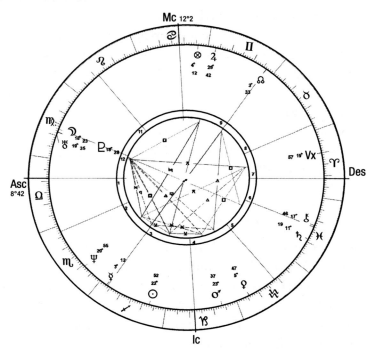

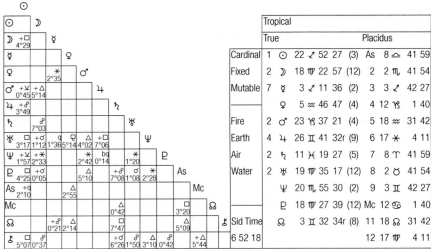

RESOURCES AND RECOMMENDATIONS FOR CHAPTER 2

Astrology

The birth chart or horoscope is a picture or snapshot of the heavens when observed from a certain point on the Earth, and the picture changes every few minutes. That is why it is unique and can clearly show exactly what it is you came to Earth to be and do. When it's interpreted from your soul's perspective, it's very illuminating and can help you to understand more of your life path and journey.

As Carl Jung who studied and worked with astrology said: *"Whatever is born or done this moment of time, has the qualities of this moment of time."*

So in a nutshell;

> *The horoscope can be viewed as a school in which the lessons of life are learned.*

> *There are twelve houses in the horoscope and each relates to a different area of your life.*

> *The twelve houses represent the classrooms.*

> *The signs, i.e. Aries through to Pisces, describe the lessons you came to learn.*

> *The planets are the teachers; e.g. Pluto is the planet of transformation and when it aspects your chart it creates or mirrors major shifts in your life. It also describes how and where you will go through transformation in your life.*

So how can astrology shed light on your divine potential and sacred path?

The three most important factors in understanding your life purpose and divine potential are:

The rising sign (Ascendant), which is calculated by the moment you take your first breath at birth!

The chart ruler(s) (soul centred and personality rulers) and their placement and aspects.

The north and south node.

These can only be worked out from an accurate birth chart and not from sun sign astrology.

One of the most empowering ways of viewing astrology and your birth chart is to see it as a mirror of the synchronistic events occurring in your external world.

Richard Tarnos, author of *Cosmos and Psyche* and *Passion of the Western Mind,* views it as a profound method to understand how you as an individual fit into the whole.

Big synchronicities often happen with life crisis, births and deaths or when falling in love. They do happen regularly at other times in life but often we only pay attention to the big ones and miss the smaller ones.

Astrology is very useful as it can make you more consciously aware of synchronicities, what they mean once you understand more about your birth chart, and view the planetary movements as a dance that is highlighting them for you in your life! That is what makes it such a profound tool in living at a higher consciousness level and making sure you do not miss opportunities. Therefore, pay attention and you will learn from the gift it offers you. *It's an interactive and dynamic mirror of how you are being acted on by the Universe and your role in the expansion of yourself!*

So let us look at this in more detail and start with the houses.

Houses. The twelve houses are like twelve classrooms you move through in your life and each one offers a different arena for your learning.

Signs. There are twelve of them too, and they are the lessons; so we look at which houses are occupied and at the planets, as each one of them is the 'teacher' (i.e. Sun, Moon, Mercury, Venus, Mars, Jupiter, Saturn, Uranus, Pluto and Chiron); we also look within the houses, as this will show the backdrop or stage for your experience. For example, if you have Sun in Aries in your seventh house, you will learn how to assert (Aries) yourself (Sun) through your most intimate relationships (seventh).

So Aries will have lessons on assertion.

The Sun is the teacher of how you express your individuality.

The seventh house will be the classroom and this rules intimate relationships and marriage.

In a birth chart, the twelve houses are described briefly as follows:

First house, relates in the natural zodiac to Aries, personality expression, ego, the mask that you wear to the world and appearance, environment, and soul's purpose.

Second House, rules Taurus and is concerned with your money, values, talents, sense of self-worth, and security.

Third House, rules Gemini and is the arena of communication, education, lower mind of the personality, and speech.

Fourth House, the very root of your chart naturally rules Cancer, which is concerned with your inherited characteristics, your home and family, roots, childhood heritage, and father image (or hidden parent).

Fifth House, rules Leo and governs creativity, children, love, romance and lovers, recreation and fun.

Sixth House and the natural home to Virgo, is concerned with the area of work, health, self-purification, daily routine and tasks, habits, service, and pets.

Seventh House is the one opposite your ascendant sign and show who you are not. It naturally rules Libra and is the classroom to look at for lessons in relationships, marriage and/or business partnerships, your awareness of others and even open enemies!

Eighth House is the ruler of Scorpio and overlooks your partner's values, whether in marriage or business, money, sex, death and transformation, crisis, or regeneration.

Ninth House rules Sagittarius and is concerned with your philosophy, belief systems, higher education, travel, higher consciousness and the very beliefs that hold your world together.

Tenth House rules Capricorn, and this is the sign of initiation, status, goals, destiny, career, mother image, social values – life direction and highest potential.

Eleventh House rules Aquarius and is related to group awareness, social conscience and service, hopes and wishes, friends and –groups – like twitter!

Twelfth House relates to Pisces, which is the last sign of the zodiac and is concerned with dissolution of the ego into the oneness of life, unconscious, hidden strengths and weaknesses, spirituality, sacrifice, past-lives, surrender experiences and miracles.

We all have to learn lessons in these twelve classrooms, depending on where your planets land in your own birth chart. That is either natal i.e. when you were born, or by transit, which is when a planet apparently spends time in the classroom to teach you a specific lesson. Transits will give an indication of the lessons you are working on in your life and at this point in time, which are encouraging you to grow and thus to help you evolve!

The soul's purpose for incarnating

The soul incarnates in each of the twelve signs of the zodiac many times to unfold its qualities. The soul sends a part of itself (the personality) into the lower worlds of existence for the purpose of gaining new experiences and thereby expressing and developing its latent qualities. To make contact with the soul, the personality must begin to tread the spiritual path and seek to re-connect with the spiritual part of it, which can lead it home to its source. We have come from the *One Source* and become the many and through love, wisdom and magnetic attraction we learn about ourselves and are lead home to the One – the divine source. This occurs through love and relationships and helps us to heal the opposite qualities (dualities) inherent within us so that we are whole (again).

This may occur after one undergoes a period of difficulty or 'soul searching' and a deeper need to understand one's life occurs. As soon as we start searching for answers or look out with our previous boundaries of belief, we begin to tap into a higher level of power that can assist us. Some people call this God or feel it is a higher power or spirit. In essence, it is irrelevant what we call it, as it is really our own inner power and love (which is within our own soul) that is available to us, if we are willing to tune into it and follow its wisdom and guidance. This often leads us to meet with the 'right' person at the 'right' time or to have coincidences, which propel our lives in a new direction. It also connects us to the guides and angels, which are operating in another invisible dimension, but are always available if we ask them to help us.

Each person's soul has a part (or soul's purpose) to play in the divine plan for humanity; the more evolved and conscious you become, the more you can tap into this for guidance and access previously unavailable resources or help. The rising sign or ascendant can identify the purpose and intention of the soul. An accurate time of birth is essential to calculate this point as it changes sign every two hours. Once we have calculated this point, you can say that this is the first house or sector and place the other twelve houses in a circle in an anti-clockwise direction. You are then able to ascertain which area the planets fall in and the emphasis or life pattern is in place. It is a blueprint and although it may appear that you are fated to have certain experiences, you always have the ability to flow with your destiny and inner divinity or to obstruct or challenge it. Thus, you have free will to choose to grow through joy and release struggle. This can be an important turning point!

Ultimately, you are here on Earth to become the master of your own destiny and understand that the lessons you are learning are for your highest good and were chosen by your soul so that you could be empowered to experience all you came to do in your Sacred Contract and to fulfil your destiny.

So your birth chart is a moment frozen in time – a picture of the heavens as they appeared at the time of your birth from the place of your birth. However, the planets do not remain stationary at birth; they keep moving, and as they do, they aspect other planets and angles in your birth chart or they return to where they were at birth, thus triggering the potential inherent within the chart. The birth chart is a map of your psyche or the seed from which all our potential can flow. The unfolding occurs under the transits and progressions, which are indicators of the timing of your seed's evolution.

Each of you is in a continual process of unfolding and the birth chart can put you in touch with the higher plan for your life or the bigger picture as seen and co-created by the higher part of our being. To work creatively and positively with this wiser part of your being, you have to believe that all your lessons are being meted out by your own soul (which is intimately connected to your inner divinity) to help you to grow and evolve into the beautiful being you already are, deep within and know ourselves as divinity incarnated. Therefore, expanding your consciousness is one of the main purposes of astrology. It is not about fortune telling or being psychic. It is about listening and observing your inner world and all the outer events occurring in your life. You can then relate this to the birth chart and the symbolic language and story it depicts of your unfolding life. Astrology and the symbols correctly interpreted can be a positive and useful guide to your higher path and enable you to see your life from a much higher perspective than you may normally view it.

The planets that create the most obvious changes in your life are Jupiter, Saturn, Uranus, Neptune and Pluto. Each of these planets has a different effect on your psyche and according to some mystics including Edgar Cayce, this is due to the fact that we have all spent time in-between lives attuning to their vibrations. Thus, when these planets and their particular vibrations affect you, you remember your time spent learning in its sphere during a spiritual sojourn. And having already agreed to be tested in certain ways, you can reach up to your soul and request help and direction in facing challenges and important transformations.

Transits and progressions

A transit is the movement of a planet through the zodiac relative to the planets and house cusps in the birth chart. It is the trigger and can release the potential inherent within you, as it aspects significant planets or angles. As it sounds, these have important transitory effects on your consciousness during the time they are around you, which can be up to two years in the case of Pluto and Neptune.

These transits often move back and forth over a given planet or angle and, slowly but surely, you learn the lessons you have agreed to and undergo changes in your consciousness.

Transits tend to bring new people and experiences into our lives.

Progressions are changes of consciousness within and indicate the life pattern and trends within a person. They correspond to the theory that one day of life symbolises one year of life as appears prophetically in the Bible: "I assign you, a day for each year."(Ezekiel: 4:6)

Progressions are seen as life indicators for marriage, births, house/job changes, and endings or deaths etc., as they tend to correlate with important outer events, which occur to mirror the psychological inner changes.

A brief description of the outer planets and their actions

Jupiter is the planet of expansion and growth. It is usually felt to be a very positive and beneficial influence in our lives. It spends one year in each sign of the zodiac and takes twelve years to transit round the whole chart. Whatever area Jupiter is affecting can bring growth, expansion, 'good fortune' and an attunement to the part of you, which is in touch with the divine, and thus, your own wisdom and faith. It therefore encourages you to take risks and gives us more confidence and trust in the process of life. Jupiter can at times exaggerate or emphasise areas of your personality, which need to be redefined positively for our growth. In doing this it can accentuate difficulties initially so that you will take action to change. Every eleven to twelve years you receive a new influx of energy to your 'Sun' sign or ascendant sign when Jupiter moves through it.

Saturn is the cosmic schoolteacher who insists that you learn all your soul lessons properly and do not avoid or try to escape from your Karma (or whatever we have created in the past and may not have accepted full responsibility for at the time). It spends 2 ½ years in each sign and takes 28–30 years to travel round the whole chart. When it returns to this point (at age 29 approximately), it is called the Saturn return and it is seen to be a very important time of psychological adjustment for everyone. It signifies the maturation process of our ego and is symbolic of your coming of age astrologically. You are ready to start a new 30-year cycle at this time and are often freed from Karmic bonds, which you brought in with you at birth. This is an important time to accept who you are under all the programmes or Karmic veils, which you may have unconsciously lived out to gain other peoples' approval. At the age of 59, you again have a period of review and can often see how far you have come in the last 30 years.

You may also be aware that you still have much work to do to free yourself of anything, which is standing in the way of you reaching your higher purpose. Saturn is associated with your ego and shadow part of your psyche and can place limits or restrictions on your life in the area it is affecting, so that you can learn your lessons and move forward as more rounded individuals. It can sometimes exacerbate your fears and make you feel more despondent about your life as it gives you a reality check on planet Earth.

Uranus is the planet of revolutionary change and excitement. It loves to breathe new life into your life and wake you up to who you are under the Karmic veils and to new directions in your life. It tends to enliven and encourage you to take risks and shock you out of old habits and life patterns, which are long past their sell by date! It speeds up change in your life and brings whatever was just below the level of your consciousness up to the surface, thus it is often called the awakener. When it makes important aspects to your charts, you often have flashes of insight or revelations about your path and purpose. The underlying excitement and sense of prophecy, which accompanies these moments, can sustain you over time as you tread the path towards your higher purpose and destiny. It is the planet associated with intuition and inner-knowing. It makes significant aspects at age 21 for everyone and is associated with the midlife crisis (at age 40–41 approximately) when you often alter your life, as it no longer seems appropriate to your needs or core self. It spends seven years in each sign and takes 84 years to travel round the birth chart.

Neptune is the planet of illusion and dreams and tends to spiritualise your life in a big way. It is associated with divine discontent and puts you in touch with your urge for perfection, the sublime and enlightenment. It often causes you to feel disillusioned as a means of leading you out of your self-imposed prison of illusion and thus putting you in touch with your own inspiration and spirituality. It is often prominent at times of peak experiences or when you fall in love; it helps you to be reunited with source and unconditional love for all life. It encourages you to merge with something greater than yourself and dissolves boundaries in your life. It is associated with art, music and all forms of creative self-expression, which help you to be in the moment and express love. It spends fourteen years in each sign of the zodiac and takes 165 years to complete one revolution of your chart.

Pluto is the planet associated with birth, death and rebirth. It transforms your life completely and often leads you to surrender to a higher power as you learn how to use power for good or otherwise. It often creates power struggles, either between yourself and other people, or with the divine and how you perceive fate, destiny or Karma. Its lessons are about non-attachment and the ability to let go, thus it is often aspecting your charts when you undergo the major rites of passage in your life, e.g. births, deaths and transformation through marriage, health or career etc. You die to your old way of life or old identity and are reborn during Pluto transits. Sometimes these endings are painful and cause you to hold on to the known. It often feels like the hand of God or fate touching you as you learn humility and how to acquiesce to the wiser part of your being that knows what is for your highest good in life. At other times, you are able to appreciate and flow with these changes and enjoy the new life you create through your own desire for transformation at a more conscious level. It spends 15–25 years in each sign of the zodiac and takes 248 years to complete one full revolution of a chart.

All the planets move sequentially through the signs from Aries to Pisces. The outer planets move fairly slowly and will affect you most significantly when they aspect one of your planets or angles. Since these outer planets remain so long in each sign (particularly Uranus, Neptune and Pluto), whole generations are affected by their subtle actions at a collective and individual level.

Once you view the planets as cosmic teachers, which are both within you (as energies and vibrations) and around you, you can co-operate with them and understand that they are helping you to reach your highest potential each time they aspect your chart in an important manner.

Dream work and journalling

Have you ever wondered if your dreams are linked to your Destiny?

We spend about one third of our lives asleep and a fair chunk of that time is occupied by our dreams.

Of that time we may have a few 'big dreams' that are related to our sacred purpose that can give us guidance that we should heed. Other dreams may also be significant but on a more mundane level!

So how do we distinguish between the normal 'filing' kind of dream in which nothing of any great note occurs and those that are truly portentous.

Often just by paying attention and starting a dream journal these more significant dreams can be called forth. Like everything in life, when we pay attention to something and offer it greater reverence it often magically shifts, allowing new insights, inklings or miracles to occur. So if you have never tried dream journalling, and want to learn more about what the divine is up to in shaping your life, then that is one of my first suggestions.

☞ Buy a journal and mark it 'Dream Journal'. Write down its purpose on the inside cover and what you hope to achieve by having it. Have a dedication ceremony and sign your declaration to honour yourself and your dreams.

☞ You can also keep some notes of events, thoughts and feelings, which were occurring when you bought it, plus any significant dreams that seem to be linked, thus combining a spiritual journal with the dreams.

☞ Be sure to choose something that you feel chimes in with your unconscious mind or something that draws an emotion or feeling, rather than just a cheap notebook. Like everything in life, what you value and show reverence for will in some way reflect this back to you and your world.

Every time I have ever chosen to do this or been guided to do so – the same thing happens. Dreams show up in my life that seem to be laden with guidance and offer me support and nurturing, even if externally life seems chaotic.

As all great mystics and spiritual seekers know, life can be chaotic externally, especially at times of expansion into your greater soul self. However, it is no reason to lose the plot internally when you have help and guidance as to why it may be occurring. That is not to say it is always comfortable; having a strong spiritual connection and working on your inner landscapes can bring a new slant and beauty to your waking life that many are completely unaware of!

Here are some ideas and prompts for you in working with your dreams:

☞ Before you fall asleep, ask for guidance on an area of your life that is important for you right now.

☞ You can even record the question and request guidance on paper.

☞ If you use astrology, be aware of your transits and cycles – or if you are not – get a consultation from someone you trust to help you understand what is happening at the unconscious level through your birth chart!

☞ When you wake, replay the dream in your mind so that you catch it all and record it as soon as you can.

☞ Keep a torch, paper, and pen by the bed – you can transfer the information later to your journal!

☞ Note what key emotion(s) or charge were associated with the dream – this is very important!

☞ Was the dream in colour or black and white?

☞ What was the dream about and who/what did you recognise in it – remember symbology is key!

☞ Write down the key events, themes and images.

☞ What Archetypes showed up in your dream?

☞ What message(s) or feeling(s) did you receive from the dream?

Once you have all this information, start to relate it to the question or issue you have been working with. Examine whether the dream affords a quick answer – often they do and there is no great need for lengthy interpretations. Other times you may need to work on the dream and tease out what each symbol or key event means for you. Once you have an answer, reflect on what action you need to take next! This way you are showing your higher self that you can be guided and will indeed follow your inner guidance. If this is in conflict with others, or even with your own rational mind, you can be sure it is worth exploring and following.

Over the next few days be alert to any further guidance and record this in your journal. By doing this you become aware of your dream life and see how it can add greater meaning to daily events and people who show up in your world. Coincidences may multiply and synchronicities often seem to occur when I do this!

Write a summary of the findings and then once you feel this is complete, you can move on to a new topic.

Review this on a regular basis and keep your spiritual journals, dream journal and birth charts together as you may want to cross-reference them at turning points in your life. This may be a time when you have a 'big dream' or receive any new revelations about your life purpose. Often the bigger picture needs time to form the beautiful mosaic-like jigsaw that it is – YOU – to become bigger by working at this level allowing the richness of the divine's hand to show up and guide you in your life! Moreover, you are able to see the beauty of all life and your unique role in a new light!

Although you may not want to do this all the time, setting aside short periods when you can have extra sleep or reflection may be beneficial and allow your creativity and destiny to blossom in ways you might never have imagined!

You may also find the information on Neptune in Chapter one helpful, as it rules dreams in astrology.

Read *Sacred Contracts* by Caroline Myss, as a companion to this book.

Caroline Myss describes a Sacred Contract as a bond, a woven thread between two souls that holds the potential of awakening a pathway to the sacred within you. Two people transform each other's lives because they ignite something in each other.

The lover Archetype and planet Venus as keys to your treasure.

The lover asks: "What would you love to do?" The challenge is, what love would do is hardly ever what security would do. For love, you will risk everything for your deepest held values!

Values – the lover is the archetype of your values.

Some questions and ideas to ponder

☞ What do you love to do?

☞ What are you willing to live for, what are you willing to die for? What are you willing to focus all of your attention on (even if it requires a life that if others looked at it, without your inner knowledge, they would see as one of sacrifice and hardship at times)?

☞ This is what fills your heart and fills you with a sense of purpose. And to make the choice to go with this, with your passion – and how the passion can serve and empower others, you have to work through the second chakra and become empowered.

☞ Venus is the ruler of Libra and Taurus in astrology. It is closely related to love, money, talents and relationships.

☞ Explore Venus in your natal birth chart by house placement and aspects to discover how it is supporting you to live out your Lover Archetype and how it can transform one of the four Universal Archetypes, the prostitute (guardian of faith) into your lover.

Diagram 2 – My Sacred Contract
Chart of Origin – Gill Potter – March 2009

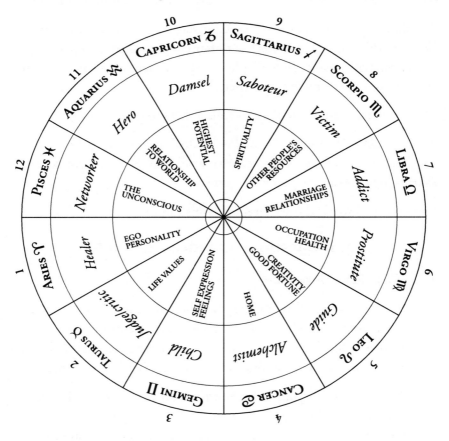

Archetypal Wheel

Chapter 3

THE INNER JOURNEY

Breakthrough

Between 1992 and 1998, I was really on an intense inner journey of self-discovery! I started to write and document my journey around my own Moon sign in my astrology chart.

You see I was born with my natal Moon in the earthy sign of Virgo, exactly conjunct to Pluto (planet of transformation) and Uranus (planet of revolutionary change and excitement) in my twelfth house of mystical transformation and surrender. It's called a Satellium in astrology, and means that the fate of these three bedfellows is intimately connected and will always be so for me! The sign of Virgo rules health and purification, so I knew that my desired healing required a sound examination of my Moon.

An excerpt from my Tune Into Your Moon programme

Moon in Virgo: You are very sensitive, cautious, and shy about showing others your feelings. Though you may love and care for someone a great deal, you rarely express those feelings openly and freely. You have a strong analyst within you and can be discriminating, which can serve you but may at times cause you to be overly judgemental. Very often, your love for someone will be expressed by trying to help them, doing something tangible to benefit them, or serving them in some way. It is also difficult for you to receive warmth, affection, or appreciation, for you often feel that you do not really deserve it or that "they don't really mean it". You can therefore seem rather cool and aloof, much more so than you feel. A deeply ingrained critical attitude can make you difficult to live with. You need to learn to be gentler and less of a perfectionist with others and with yourself. Try to accept flaws as part of the human condition.

Moon in 12th house: You may be a bit of a secretive person and find your own feelings and emotions to be something of an enigma – even to you! It is often difficult for you to share with others what you are feeling. You frequently withdraw from contact with the world, and need a healing, peaceful environment in order to blossom and come out of yourself. You identify with the oppressed, disenfranchised or underdog in any situation. Service and caring for those in need is very important and you are often found working behind the scenes. You may keep a journal or write as an outlet for feelings that you can be consumed by.

So I decided it was time to really go and investigate myself and excavate my inner self, and I continued to work on being my own counsellor in February 1998!

Self-healing

11/2/98
I compiled a list of all the things I had criticised myself for at that point or that I had done consistently through my life. This ranged from being ill and not being in control of my life to being very needy. I ended up with a list of seventeen – not surprising with my Moon in Virgo. I also looked at all the labels I had attached to myself, like I'm too ill, I'm too frightened of failure – I discovered ten. Based on this, I took a long hard look at how much I did not support myself and made a contract up, which included a vow of confirmation to support myself and start afresh.

Try it – it is highly recommended!

For the next few days, I was ill with migraines and what seemed to be another severe relapse of my M.E. and therefore, I remember feeling a lot of despair once again! Often this is the way of change – we take a big leap forward only to be stopped in our tracks and are required to love ourselves despite the difficulties. So I did -I nursed myself through this difficult time and listened to my inner child's fears. I sent her love and opened my heart in a way I never had thought possible and I prayed for a miracle – and then things really began to shift! I was guided to read my medical dictionary, as I was feeling so giddy and had dreadful vertigo, and I found this entry close to one on vertigo – only my soul or God could have directed me to it!

Vertebrobasilar Insufficiency

Syndrome caused by lack of blood to the hindbrain. May be progressive, episodic or both. Clinical manifestations include giddiness and vertigo, nausea, ataxia, drop attacks and signs of cerebellar disorder such as nystagmus.

The lights went on immediately and I knew this was it! The answer or at least part of it had appeared – at last! I made an appointment to see my GP (who had always been very supportive but had no idea what else to do with me!). I was on the maximum amount of anti-depressants at this time – 150 mgs of prothiaden and had been given up as a hopeless case. I was on Incapacity Benefit and had been given disability living allowance more or less for life. Money and security were taken care of, but my life and youth were going down the toilet and fulfilling my highest potential was as far away as it possibly could be at that time!

I took the dictionary with me and explained that I had a severe migraine with all of the above symptoms. She took my blood pressure and it was through the roof as my head was so painful and the breathlessness had been getting worse over the winter.

She then prescribed Propranolol and I just knew that I was going to get better. She also referred me to see a neurologist, and said she thought I was right! I felt like jumping for joy!

This was my first BIG breakthrough of many breakthroughs in healing my body (my healing journey had started years before!). It gave me a lot of trust in myself and my soul, as well as the feeling that I was being guided and a miracle was happening – at last!

I wrote this after my visit to the Doctor.

25/2/98

> *A small flame flickers*
> *In the distance*
> *Offering new hope and opportunity*
> *But I step back*
> *Observing silently*
> *Afraid to breathe*
> *For fear of extinguishing this light*
> *A new dawn awaits*
> *Seven years have passed*
> *Until at last the fates*
> *Have suddenly chosen this moment*
> *To illuminate the path*
> *The jigsaw may at last*
> *Come together and justify the past*
> *Of fear and pain and despair*
> *But still I am so afraid to believe*
> *That this nightmare can be outcast*
> *I pray and hope for faith*
> *To get me through these long days*
> *The final hours of waiting*
> *For my sentence to be read*
> *My fate to be sealed*
> *Unsure of which way to swing*
> *To hope or fear*
> *To joy or tears*

And so gradually things started to improve on the new medication and I had hope – at last. Even better, I started to be able to walk again! The pain that I had experienced every time I tried to walk reduced and the medication started to open up my brain allowing more oxygen to circulate. Sounds simple and crazy that it had never been detected before – but it had not! The dream work I had done throughout 1994 with my Moon had been right. I knew from those dreams that somehow, someway, I would get well and had always held that firm belief – finally it seemed that it could come true and I could get my life back!

Tune into your Moon

In astrology, the Moon is very important, especially in a woman's chart as it shows your instincts, intuition, receptivity and perceptions. The lunar cycle lasts approximately 29.5 days and affects us all emotionally, showing different periods of creative impulses, urge for restoration and reflection.

Working with your inner child and identifying the patterns that you learned in childhood can address how you are now aligned with your emerging divinity and how best to support and nurture it. She is your guardian of innocence and by working with the Child Archetype, you awaken a new relationship with your life that can allow you to flow in tandem with your natural inner cycle and tap into your creative impulses that may have been dormant. Confronting her and making her your ally will support you to become a positive source of nourishment for yourself and clients, friends and family. In this way, you transform her from being a drain on your resources to being the source of your inner strength, thus bringing the sensation and inner knowing that all things are possible!

November 2009 was the next time when I would really start working with my own Moon and inner child at an even deeper level than ever before! I attended two workshops at Findhorn on healing and have to say that they caused me to look at my past through a new lens. This is not something I can say I truly wanted to go back and do! Nevertheless, it was time! It felt more like a necessity to be honest. In addition, I have learned on my journey of healing that pain and pleasure are inextricably linked – divine paradox!

It was a cathartic few days, almost like going back to where it all began and looking at my life through new eyes; a fresh perspective that helped me to clear out the remaining debris and buried grief from past events.

The first workshop was by Caroline Myss and looked at the "simple truths that can heal your life". I found that as I went through the three days, any sense of injustice and entitlement around certain issues began to dissipate. The realisation that everything we have is a gift and that we are entitled to nothing really sank in. I was able to be grateful for the many miracles that occurred when I was at Findhorn, that I might have seen just as happy coincidences otherwise! Two examples are listed below:

I arrived running a bit late on the Saturday around lunchtime. I had driven from my hometown of East Kilbride to Forres, which is a three and a half hour drive and had a lot of luggage to carry up to my room. I was allocated my room, which was on the top floor (three flights up) to share with two others from the course. So collecting my suitcase and bags from my car I stood at the bottom of the stairs considering how best to proceed. Almost immediately someone appeared from nowhere by my side and offered to help me. I thanked them saying they were like an angel in disguise, and as I was on the top floor, I was grateful that they had been sent to help me. I didn't give this too much thought until we did the exercise on entitlement and was relating that I hadn't looked for anyone to help me (which I hadn't), as I was intent on helping myself to get up the stairs with my luggage. My friend who was doing the exercise said the opposite. She had been hoping for someone to help her but no one came and she felt a bit miffed by this! That intrigued me and made me look at some of the things I do (and did) feel entitled to. Often, it is the very things that I focus on as lacking that cause my greatest sense of not being looked after; whereas, the things I just decide I can do, often seem to throw up extra help and kindness.

The second example is that at Findhorn many of the workshops attendees are assigned tasks to carry out whilst there. The last time I went, I had not been assigned any but my two friends had (to help with washing up etc.). I felt glad, as being a nurse at one time, I have spent a lot of my life doing less than savoury tasks for patients. So again, when I had this discussion with my roommates at dinner it turned out that they both had been assigned tasks, but I had been given none. I looked on this as divine grace in a way, since I have never had a big issue about service in these ways!

Now on to the bigger issues of healing and reverence.

James Finley in the second of the two workshops spoke about having "reverence for your wounds". He offered the metaphor of saving the child (that you know is trapped in there) from a burning building to allow the divine gifts we have all been born with to be fully claimed and used in service to others. Suddenly I had tears running down my face and the sense that I was in exactly the right place again to heal what is ready to be healed.

So it became obvious to me that it was time to revisit the wound, not to indulge it or use it as manipulation as so many do to control others in their life, but just to honour my own life and path and fulfil my desire to be of greater service to others.

It is not an easy path but the alternative, as Caroline Myss so succinctly describes in the aforementioned book, is one of attachment to wounds that serve oneself and manipulate others.

So why is it so hard for us all to give up wounds?

Well one reason is that we know without a doubt that our lives will change. If we let go of certain things including our wounds, life has to change. And the reality is we are often more afraid of change than of death. We are controlled by our wounds and we control others by our wounds.

Finding your sacred path through healing is indeed a worthy quest!

RESOURCES AND RECOMMENDATIONS FOR CHAPTER 3

Quiz – How well do you know yourself?

On a scale of 1–100 where would you be? Let's say 1 is not at all and 100 is divine consciousness and self-realisation.

Just for fun where do you 'feel' you are right now? Quantify it or ask yourself again.

How well do I know myself?

So you might know what foods you like or the clothes shops you enjoy buying from or what brand of lipstick suits you!

But of course I'm thinking here of more deeply knowing yourself!

So I'll ask again – how well do you truly know yourself?

I wonder how many times you have stopped and realised that you do not truly know the answer to that question, (yet) nor may you ever! Perhaps it is a new thought for you and you have to consider if, by even answering it how it might change your life if you did!

How that one choice will fit in with who you are or who you are becoming as distinct from your personality desires for you! Life is simply a series of choices and decisions based on who you believe you are right now!

Spiritual growth is a bit like that. If we just stayed in the old and stuck ways then we keep answering questions habitually because they tend to be the same ones.

What time will I get up? – 7 a.m.

How will I get to work? – by car.

Who will I meet at work? – same people I always meet and so on.

We become like mini programmers and do not allow space for the new to emerge, relinquishing our true identity under lots of daily 'to do lists' and 'keep others happy' lists.

That has been my experience of anyone who does not really want to know themselves. They bury their potential far from view and plod along – sometimes happily, sometimes unhappily – for many years or even a lifetime!

To know yourself takes courage, determination, and the willingness to make mistakes. It means taking new actions, or being at peace with inaction, meeting new people and seeking out opportunities and experiences that were all in your energy field but are latent until the light is shone on them. It means being willing to change, to look in the mirror and love what you see or if you do not, by taking steps to rectify this.

Spiritual growth shines the light on everything that is ready to surface. A bit like the planet Uranus, it revolutionises your life by waking you up to your true identity and allows the old patterns, beliefs and negativity to fall away. With that awakening, many of the more material aspects of life change too. Letting go of homes, loved ones, clothes, names and titles... sometimes the letting go seems to go on forever. You might even cry a lot more and feel emotional – sensing the old you is being released – an ego death!

However, there is a point when you know you have shed all you can – for now. You feel empty – not in a sense of loss – just empty of everything that was blocking you being YOU! Some books describe it as dissolving into holiness and allowing you to be more whole. In Buddhist teaching, 'emptiness' refers to a basic openness and no separation that we experience when all fixed and small notions of yourself dissolve allowing you to live in peace and harmony.

That is when the real you can shine through.

Divine consciousness seeks newness. It seeks love and to be loved more as a natural side effect because it simply is love. It knows no boundaries, wears no airs and graces, and wants to live and let live with peace and harmony. It manifests naturally through seeking out a similar vibration, follows intuition and trusts in miracles. It is aware of the oneness that all true power is spiritual power, which involves aligning with the 'all that is' and what is for the highest good of all, including you.

In between, you can choose to struggle or you can choose to surrender to the force within that can carry you safely to that space. Perhaps for you it is being in nature, or meditating or simply allowing what is through acceptance? Certainly taking time to be in touch with your inner voice and knowingness is essential for anyone on a path of accelerated growth.

Stopping the inner conflict and "taking the one seat" as Jack Kornfield describes in *A Path With Heart* means having the courage to face head-on all the pettiness and negativity, and transform it through love, learning, and letting go.

The true nature of each being can shine for all to see; it is a beautiful process and outcome when it is supported, given the reverence it truly requires by you, and those around you.

So one last time, how well do you know yourself? Where are you on the scale now between 1 and 100?

If it is the same, then perhaps you need to look more deeply at how much you do not know yourself.

If it is higher up towards 100, then perhaps you realise you do know more than you let on!

Moreover, if you have dropped down the scale, then perhaps you know it is time to work on this area a bit more deeply.

Affirmation for inner peace

Just for today, I choose to be at peace, to go in peace and to walk in the light. I affirm that I will allow my life to unfold in attunement with my inner voice, knowing that is aligned with my divine self and the divine plan for my life.

Follow your intuition and let nothing stand in your way. All paths eventually lead to God and your inner divinity.

Everything else is simply a necessity, a sideshow of fun, distractions and cul-de-sacs!

Your astrological Moon as defining your inner child. The Moon rules Cancer and the fourth house of the zodiac Generally it also rules:

☞ How you nurture yourself and others

☞ Wholesome state of femaleness/motherhood

☞ Healthy instincts and a sense of safety and security

☞ Feelings of support and supply/abundance

☞ Attunement to your unconscious, intuition and divine guidance

☞ Your needs and whether or not you can meet them/feel they are met

☞ Receptivity and responsiveness to others' needs; empathy

☞ Attachments, habits and emotions

☞ Roots, home, the past and family inheritance In Sacred Contracts, the Moon is very connected to the Child Archetype and for me this is our closest connection with the divine – the point of our greatest vulnerability and also so important in our journey to be the sovereign of our life purpose and destiny!

☞ Child Archetype; Guardian of innocence

☞ The sensation that everything and anything is possible – closely connected with our core divinity and trust in that higher power.

☞ Dependency and vulnerability issues.

☞ Shadow is neediness, seeking approval, inability to care for self/ others and unable to grow up to become a mature creative adult.

Some questions to answer and reflect upon related to your inner child

Describe your childhood in 100 words or less. What role did you play in your family as a child? How has that transferred to how you are living right now? Can you draw any conclusions from your childhood that need to be addressed at this time? What age is your inner child? What quest has your inner child taken you on? What wisdom or guidance does s/he give you? How do you know when you are connected to your inner child in a healthy way?

How can you go forward now by understanding and listening to your inner child in a new way ? How does your inner child protect or alert you to danger?

Transforming the Child Archetype into your Sovereign

Your Child Archetype is transformed into the Sovereign via the hero's journey. Just as Dorothy in the Wizard of Oz (innocent child) sets off to meet the powerful wizard, whom she believes can get her back to her home, family and security, so we all have to make that journey into our deepest insecurities and address how to become empowered – for both ourselves and our tribe! The innocent child within you needs to learn to trust in intuition and instincts and be open to the support and guidance as you walk your own yellow brick road (think light aspects of your psyche) and learn about self-mastery.

Tuning into your Moon can support you in this journey; so explore your Moon by sign, house and aspect in your birth chart, and start healing and loving your inner child in a new way.

Chapter 4

LOVE IS THE ANSWER

1988 began with me working as a staff nurse at Falkirk Royal Infirmary. I was alone and depressed in a two-bedroom ex-council flat, with only my beloved Ginger and white kitten Tigger for company. I felt trapped and at only 22, I felt like I was on Dead End Street.

I was tired of living a seemingly purposeless life, paying bills and felt swamped in depression. So I looked for a way out from this mess of lack of money and feeling unfulfilled emotionally. So I prayed, went to church and searched for answers, got drunk, smoked cigarettes and cried.

One night in February 1988, I got excessively drunk when out with my boyfriend at a friend's house. In trying to coerce a marriage proposal out of him, I ended up causing us to fall out. This in turn freed me to make new choices that were much more supportive of what I needed!

We broke up. I sold my flat. I was offered a place to do my RSCN training at Yorkhill. I discovered a group to study astrology. And I moved to the fashionable West end of Glasgow.

Hurrah – success!

My new life began!

I remember buying my first car in March 1988 (I had passed my test in October 1987), and loved driving along at high speeds with the music blaring. I would sing my heart out and was overjoyed to be free from the shackles of responsibility that the previous two years had brought. I no longer had a boyfriend but I actually felt like I was finding myself for the first time and that the despair I felt I had buried could be exorcised. I was feeling hopeful, optimistic that life could be good!

The anxiety attacks that I had suffered periodically for eight years were no longer troublesome and I was much more confident. I decided it was time to reinvent myself. I had more money as going to train as a sick children's nurse meant I was still paid as a staff nurse with the luxury of being able to study with a lot less responsibility.

Reinventing myself

I bought lots of new clothes and began to look at getting fit and healthy. Running was all the rage and my sister and brother-in-law encouraged me to take it up. I joined a running club and went out every few days. It felt good and I was in one of my non-smoking phases. Even getting drunk was less appealing.

I knew I had two weeks holiday in July as part of my sick children's nurse training, so I asked my friends what they were doing for holidays. It turned out that Lesley and Allison were already booked for Corfu with three others. There was no room at their apartment, but then I thought I could go with another nurse friend called Anne.

It all happened really fast. From moving to Glasgow on the 16th May to booking this holiday, everything just slotted into place with so much ease and grace. The two weeks holiday to Kavos in Corfu would commence on Monday the 4th July 1988 (my Grandmother's birthday).

I remember just thinking that I would plan ahead after the holiday. I had no idea what life had in store for me and in many ways, I was living in the moment!

At times, I felt some trepidation – it was all so new to be on my own with no boyfriend – to make my own decisions and choices without consulting anyone else, but it was fun and spontaneous too!

The training programme was to last sixteen months originally and part of it required health screening. I went along to occupational health at the start of June 1988, having been told it was mandatory that I have a hepatitis B injection. I was cool with that, though they did insist on telling me some of the risk factors and I had to choose between a live and a dead vaccine. I chose one of them (the one they recommended) and I remember getting the shot in my arm and going back to the oncology ward I was working in. I thought no more about it than having a routine visit to the dentist. In working for the medical services, it was all so regimented and I knew the score.

Yuppie flu

Around the same time, I was watching Wogan (a popular early evening chat show in the UK) and saw Clare Francis being interviewed. She had sailed round the world single handed and was known as a very courageous and feisty lady. It turns out though, that she has some weird virus called yuppie flu or M.E. I had never heard of such a thing and listened as she described in detail how this illness had taken her from being a top sportswoman who commanded the utmost respect to being weak and a quivering wreck at the thought of writing a letter. It had affected her body and mind and she had slept for weeks and then had to learn how to rehabilitate herself very slowly from the effects of this virus over the next two years or so. She was a lot better now – hence her appearance on TV talking about overcoming the illness. I remember thinking that it sounded so weird. Well maybe it was my soul speaking to me that day and I was being prepared – I do not know for sure – I just remember it all happened around the same time!

In fact, years later I would discover that the original meaning of the word *weird* is one who knows her destiny. That's right, being weird means to know what is right for you – so perhaps having M.E. was a necessary part of my destiny path or dharma!

The other thing I remember was watching the concert for Nelson Mandela's birthday party. He was still in prison – a political prisoner in South Africa – and the concert was raising awareness of his plight and his fight against apartheid.

'Free Nelson Mandela!' was the cry and I watched the concert and sang along to all the great songs. I loved these events like Live Aid – somehow they spoke to me of a community and connection that occurs when collaborations for the greater good are created!

Last but not least was the Glenn Medeiros song that I watched just before I left for the holiday that would change my life and destiny for ever – *Nothing's Gonna Change My Love For You!* – it has to be one of the cheesiest songs ever but I just remember watching the video, all about a holiday romance and thinking it all looked idyllic. At the same time, my main intention was to go on holiday and have fun! For once, I wanted fun with friends more than I wanted to meet the man of my dreams or have a holiday romance. I had had it up to here with all that crap! So funny when I think of it and how things unfolded over the next two weeks!

By the day of our flight, I was packed and so looking forward to be going abroad. I also seemed to be suffering from insomnia and was feeling a bit 'weird' I couldn't put my finger on it – maybe just excitement I told myself. I was tempted to drink some whisky to get my brain to shut down – it was on hyperdrive (little did I know that this was to be the start of my M.E. nightmare), I refrained but was left feeling exhausted and irritable due to the lack of sleep! After a long flight we arrived at Kavos in Corfu – it was pitch black and hot – really hot! Anne and I were a bit worse for wear; we had been up since 5 a.m., and were excited about the holiday!

We were both glad and relieved to be dispatched at our holiday apartment in Kavos. I remember Anne grumbling that it was pretty rubbish, as we had to share a fridge and a bathroom. All we had was a double room with a balcony and loads of mosquitoes to keep us company that first night. I had never experienced so many mosquitoes as this before; it was my first time in Greece and boy was it hot!!

The Holiday Romance

I first met Michael on Tuesday 5th July 1988 and the time was around midnight. Anne and I had enjoyed our first day of sunbathing in Kavos and we had even decided to go topless for the first time (which felt extremely liberating). It was to be a holiday of liberation and revelations for me; unlike anything I could ever have previously imagined.

After dinner, we decided to go and look for my other friends; Lesley and four others who were also staying in Kavos. We didn't have mobile phones back then, just the name of their apartment and a vague idea of where it was in relation to our own one.

We must have walked about a mile past lots of bars when I suddenly felt dizzy, like I was going to pass out (I now believe this was all related to the hepatitis B injection I had received four weeks previously). I said that I needed to sit down, so we entered the nearest bar – it turned out to be called *The Midnight Lady* – and we sat down. Within five minutes, a group of four guys sat down near us and soon joined us. This was Michael, his brother Calum, his cousin Jim as well as another Michael, who was Calum's friend.

Michael was the one I felt most drawn to. He had an unusual face and reminded me of an angel – a bit like Angel Clare (or the actor Peter Firth who played him in *Tess* – the Roman Polanski film). Tess was one of my all time favourite films when I had seen it in 1980. I am not sure why, but I just know that I made that connection pretty quickly.

Michael was a graphic artist and a musician who busked outside Marks and Spencer at the weekends. He had long fingernails, which fascinated me (filed and shaped, which he was very proud of – these were required to play his guitar well, apparently – and no he was not gay!) He smoked Silk Cut cigarettes (just as I did at that time) and he came from Belfast in Northern Ireland. I had such a thing for Irish accents even back then, so I was probably falling for him fast – although it was not love at first sight. We chatted and I got drunk on whisky and sprite, while he drank beer. He was a fan of The Smiths (especially Morrissey) and The Housemartins, and he told me how much he had enjoyed *Tutti Frutti* (filmed in Scotland

and on TV the year before) and *Pennies from Heaven*, which appealed to his slightly off the wall taste. My dizzy turn had resolved and eventually it was just Anne, Jim, Michael and myself. It turned out that they had been there since late Friday and would leave on the 15th July, so we had plenty of time to get to know each other better!

Well that next few hours flew by and I remember Michael and me kissing and rolling on the ground (fully clothed) and lots of people stepping over us around the bar/disco we were at. This was passion and the electricity between us was apparent! Still we all said goodnight about 5 a.m. and he and Jim (who was with Anne) didn't make any concrete plans to meet up again with us, partly because I wanted to have fun – not ties or attachments – just fun and this was just our first night in Corfu! Anne had not really fallen for Jim – so it was not really a great foursome anyway! She had just been making up the numbers.

The next few days were hot – really hot. It was about 120 degrees and people were feeling ill with the heat (in fact some people died in Greece that summer due to it).

I remember hearing about The Piper Alpha disaster and all the casualties and deaths miles away in Scotland. It was sad and I felt like I was going through a big shift myself. At one point over the next few days I lost my appetite and felt so homesick, and that I was dying that I started telling Anne about what I would leave her and everyone else in my Will. She was laughing at me but I was deadly serious. I felt like I was dying – something weird was going on inside of me!

Anyway, we had met my other friends by this time and so now we were seven girls in our early twenties out on the ran dan in Kavos and having fun, so I decided to enjoy the holiday and spent most of it pretty drunk.

I could not forget Michael though and our night of passion.

I then met another guy called Frank who was from Greenock and had a fling with him. He was besotted with me but I did not want to see him again. One night flings were not my thing but somehow too much drink and *wham bam thank you ma'am* – that is the way it happened.

I felt bad and sad that it had. Nothing to do with Frank (who was keen to see me again and heartbroken that I didn't), just too much alcohol, the effects of feeling I was about to die, and the consequences of then letting my hair down – my crazy side given full reign!

The craving to see Michael again intensified!

By Sunday evening (the 10th July) I was out and half-searching for him when I met up with his cousin, Jim. Ah – at last I thought!

"Where's Michael?" I asked.

"Don't know," he replied. "Probably off by himself. He's like that you know." I didn't, but then again it made sense. I persuaded Jim to take me back to see Michael at their apartment. I guess Jim hoped he might have a chance with me too and I even had to give him a kiss to bribe my way in. I wasn't interested in Jim, though I was a bit perplexed when he explained that Michael had a girlfriend called Sarah in Belfast. Well that was news to me, he had never mentioned it the week previously and I just thought he was single, footloose and fancy free like me!

I sat down in their apartment – on Michael's bed, and John Lennon gazed up at me – a biography of the former Beatle.

I chatted to Jim, feeling closer to Michael and we sat for about an hour. He did not appear so I agreed to meet them at the same bar – Midnight Lady – at 11 p.m. the following night, which was Monday the 11th of July.

And there he was.

That night we chatted and walked (oh and we went dancing too) and chatted and walked while the bats circled around us on one particularly dark stretch of the main road that ran through Kavos. In fact, when I think of Michael, I always remember those walks and the fact that he listened to me like no one I had ever met before. He did not interrupt, he did not judge and he did not ask stupid questions. He just listened and held my hand and it felt so good!

He was 24 and had a good sense of humour. He was not wild like me; he was calm and gentle and oh so sweet. He just laughed and said I had my "crazy head on" when I went off into my la la world!

I felt compelled to tell him everything about my life that Monday night; my past history, my Mum's illegitimacy, my recent break up with Sandy, my work as a nurse, looking after kids with cancer at Yorkhill, my unhappiness around drinking too much alcohol, my relationship history and my hopes and dreams. Everything tumbled out and he listened! It was my life story up to that point (and not something I normally shared with anyone!) and after we completed our walk, he took me back to my apartment and we kissed goodnight. There was no sex and no pressure for it either – just pure unconditional love that was like a healing, soothing balm.

The next night we met again around 11 p.m. and it was the 12th of July, when Northern Ireland goes a bit crazy over King Billy. Michael was a protestant (just like me) but he wasn't interested in sectarian claptrap either. There were a lot of people running about singing the usual sectarian songs in Kavos to celebrate it though, and it just sticks in my mind to reflect the craziness of the time.

Anyway, we left the bar and started walking again and then we met Frank and his pals. I felt a bit confused, scared even, as I did not want him to ruin my budding relationship with Michael by saying something about our fling together!

At one point while we all chatted in a group, I stepped back and felt Michael's hand clasp mine reassuringly.

That's when it happened!

This voice just spoke and said:"You're going to marry him!"

And I said: "WHAT!!!"

And it repeated the same thing.

"You're going to marry him!"

And so my mystical experience began and I was suddenly flying above us both (like an out of body experience) and looking down on us holding hands with this voice in my head telling me that I was going to marry him!

After that, everything became hazy and wonderfully exciting too. My heart (and head – or both!) felt like it had exploded and I had the sudden urge to go to the beach with Michael and follow my soul's guidance to have a mock wedding ceremony.

Michael didn't even know what was going on for me and just agreed with what I asked of him! He was totally oblivious!

It was a long sweet night of revelations and a mystical transformation unlike anything I had ever experienced.

Fourteen months later I would get married – but not to Michael!

After the ecstasy – the laundry!

Two weeks later, I was back in Glasgow! Was it all a dream? A fantastical dream! Nothing seemed real anymore in this world and the essence of the experience and events with Michael seemed like a wonderful escape valve. No one else seemed terribly interested or impressed. Just get on with your life. It was just a holiday romance. So what, if he wanted to be with you he would call or contact you. I knew this was all true – too true and too incredibly painful. They were giving me wise advice but they did not know all the facts of what had REALLY happened!

The momentous experience was my own little secret to be loved and nurtured, revisited and examined. In fact, it seemed to play through me, I walked that road a million times it seemed and then the dreams came!

I would wake up sweating having been searching for Michael. I would nearly find him, just for him to disappear out of view at the last moment. Searching searching – to no avail!

I had no plans to share my secrets with anyone – I did not want to be ridiculed. It was far too precious and sacred to bandy around and hear how no one believed me! I could just hear them tease me scornfully – well where is he then this lover boy that you are going to marry? – and of course I could only say I don't know! Because I did not understand or know what it all meant, but I was determined to find out!

I felt high those first few weeks after Corfu; high on the vibrancy of a love that I could neither forget nor release. It just hung there tantalizing me like a crystal and I would go over the events daily to examine them for new clues.

One evening after doing some ironing, I read something in one of my books.

If you desire something enough and pray for it – pray to do whatever it will take to have it then it can be yours! So I did – I prayed to God – the same God that had spoken to me that night when I had the mystical experience and I said: "I love Michael, God. You made me love him and you told me he would come back. So now I am saying I will do whatever it takes to have him back, God, to meet him again at marry him." I hugged myself with joy and fell asleep.

I woke up in a cold sweat searching, searching for him – to no avail – in my dreams!

Interspersed was life on the wards, looking after sick children and trying to move forward without understanding why it had happened and why life was now so empty without his presence and the voice too, that had been there guiding me in Corfu – all gone!

Another curious thing that was happening to me was that my body no longer followed commands or seemed to want to sleep even though I felt desperately tired. I would wake early and then try to work through intense tiredness only to have night after night of insomnia. I had been working night duty shifts so thought this might be partly to blame. Even alcohol seemed to leave me jumpy and hyperactive. Muscles twitching in my body and feelings of anxiety and unreality along with a gamut of digestive disturbances started to fill the void like a hangover from the holiday and romance. I wasn't pregnant – of that I was sure. I wished I had been! I longed to have something, anything to grasp associated with Michael. I was deeply in love and there was no one to love me back, just this dream-like demi-god and remembrance of ecstasy. I could not even blame him since he had been oblivious to much of what had gone on. It was all very perplexing and so, other than enjoying the sweet remembrance and feeling opened up to a new level of joy and possibility, I just felt discontent. Divine discontent.

Moving forward

Fortunately, my new love for astrology became part of my world at this time, as did my old love and boyfriend, Sandy!

The first time we met properly was in September 1988 – another great moment of awakening.

I had signed up for classes at the Theosophical society in Glasgow with an astrologer called Elise and was so excited that this would help me unlock the mystery related to my own life purpose and the various problems I had had with addictions, anxiety and depression, plus my panic attacks, which had started at age fourteen in school.

"Here is your birth chart," said Elise my new astrology teacher. It was beautifully hand drawn with the aspects highlighted in red and green.

I immediately flew to the three planets in the corner, as they seemed like this huge blot on the landscape – my landscape.

Immediately I labelled it as bad – the memory of panic attacks, social phobia and lack of control seemed to emanate from this – this little grouping in the 12th house; Moon, Pluto and Uranus.

Ten years later, I would write a poem by way of transforming them into my protectors rather than my prison guards who masqueraded as torturers to my soul!

I knew (just) enough at that time to have the revelation that this was the cause of much of my secret sorrows and pain.

I also felt sure astrology would shed light on my mystical experience with Michael, as I had his birth data (one of my few souvenirs) I delved into it with the passion of a modern mystic intent on her first love affair.

So the birth chart was my map, my new guide that I threw myself into to search for clues and the incessant question that plagued me – why?

Why had I met Michael, and why had he been so cruelly removed from me. Why had I been told these things? Here I thought the answers would be found. The mystery of my life would be solved with this God-given gift of astrology to me!

So while I learned my new symbolic language that would show me God's plan and make it all right, I waited with hope that Michael would return and we would marry. Then, this deep despair that pervaded my consciousness would be gone – it had to be – and I hoped and prayed that it would be soon.

Transformation and healing patterns

October came and it was now three months since these momentous events. I knew I had to move on – I was drinking more and out partying. I had somehow managed to acquire two boyfriends – neither of whom held my attention. I missed Sandy and longed for Michael. However, most of all I felt empty, devoid of drive, and this fatigue was getting worse.

I seemed to see-saw between hope and pessimism. My life was better than it had been. I liked living in Glasgow and quite enjoyed the work. I felt alone though with all this new information from my astrology books and charts roaming round my head looking for somewhere to hang my purpose.

Sandy had been in touch and I now had his chart. I was studying lots of birth charts at this time to understand astrology and how we reflected our charts. The book I had been reading by Liz Greene, Relating, was a wonderful guide to psychological astrology and our anima and animus. I seemed to have a natural talent for it and easily connected with what I was reading. Similarities between Michael's chart and Sandy's struck me and I started to feel I would like to see Sandy again. Perhaps he could shed light on my pain and my lost love. After all, I had told Michael all about him so now I could return the favour! In addition, I missed Sandy and his company.

Writing letters

Sandy and I had been writing letters for a couple of months and then I received a music tape of the Proclaimers – *Sunshine on Leith*. He wanted to see me and it seemed that I was being gently guided in that general direction. So one night working late in the wards, he turned up giving me quite a stir! We had not seen each other for a while and I immediately felt safe, like a security blanket had been offered.

Inevitably, we started to go out again and soon we were planning to marry. This time he proposed. Everything should have been wonderful – here I was marrying my long time boyfriend, planning a future together and engaging in a new hobby. It seemed all my dreams were being answered. I remembered the song *China in your Hand* and thought yes, I should be grateful and forget Michael. Therefore, I tried – I put him out of my mind and started making wedding plans. We were to marry in nine months – September 1989!

Over the winter of 1988, the strange fatigue, muscles twitching and anxiety continued. I put it down to the stress and excitement of what had been a particularly eventful year.

I was concerned and my visits to my doctor became much more frequent. All tests drew a blank. Eventually, as I was due my third hepatitis B injection, I returned to occupational health. Explaining that I felt unwell since receiving the initial hepatitis B jab and, had done so for the last few months, they seemed concerned. Perhaps you have M.E. they told me and furnished me with information about this latest weird illness that had appeared – called yuppie flu. I remembered the programme about Clare Francis and inwardly shuddered!

Anyway, I hoped it would just pass and I would get better. I had rarely been ill in my life – not physically anyway. I knew my mental health had its fragility but this was all new!

All of this chaos was the backdrop to my forthcoming wedding on the 8th September 1989.

I tried to put Michael and the momentous experience in Corfu out of my mind.

However, it played round my mind every so often, or Michael showed up in my dreams, and this made me wish for resolution and peace!

My Wedding day

8 SEPTEMBER 1989
Drawing deeply on the cigarette, I closed my eyes searching for a sense of peace and acceptance.

The dream one week before had told me it would be OK. I had awoken feeling uplifted and joyful. Mary had told me what I must do. She was my father's mother, who had passed on aged twenty; we had never met, but I had always sensed her presence in my life as a spirit guide. It was right from the first time I had taken an aversion to feathers, and was told that I was just like Mary. Perhaps she was speaking to me that day – when I was a little girl. I just knew that the dream was unusual and the feeling stayed with me for days. Here I was now about to move into alignment with her guidance and take the vows.

I stood up ready to take the next step.

"Make me a channel of your peace," the congregation sang in full voice.

I stood praying for courage to take this momentous step. Repeating my vows, I stood gazing at the new rings that now adorned my left ring finger. I was now a married woman with a new name.

The sun shone through the stained glass windows of the church marking us out; the golden couple standing at the altar.

How strange is this life I reflected and how little we know of what will be asked of us next!

"Congratulations!"

Well-wishers hugged us and we thanked them for attending our wedding. Glancing over at my new husband all seemed well – he looked flushed and happy. I silently prayed life would work out and that children and normal everyday joys would bind us together and help me forget the momentous events of last year.

Something within told me that I was doing the right thing. After all, I had wanted to get married last year and my husband's refusal had led to our break-up. I may never have gone on holiday with my friend and fallen in love with another man (or had a mystical life changing experience) if we had been together. I knew that and in many ways, it seemed natural that he had come back to me and apologised for all the hurt he had caused.

No More Lonely Nights played as our first dance and we held each other, glad to be together and wed at last.

I wrote *Bridge to my Heart* years later in honour of the journey I had related to both Sandy and Michael – my secret sorrow – and the unconditional love of my husband that kept me alive, and the care he had given to me throughout our marriage!

Bridge to my Heart – dedicated to Sandy (My Husband)

> *You are the bridge to my heart*
> *An important and necessary key to the part*
> *That unlocks the pain and the sorrow*
> *That I am unable to escape from*
> *And must face and accept with willingness and love*
>
> *You are the bridge to my heart*
> *That opens and heals the wounds of the past*
> *And helps me to release and feel the joy*
> *That I've kept locked up inside of me*
>
> *You are the bridge to my heart*
> *The reflection of my every thought*
> *The obstruction of my every dream*
> *The voice of my inner soul*
> *As you call me back from the dead*
> *And make me face all that I dread*

You are the bridge to my heart
The cruelty and the void
The compassion and the joy
The triad that makes me whole
The destruction and the resurrection

You are the bridge to my heart
The abandoned and the abused
The unconditional love and the sacrifice
The obsession and the turmoil
That I too have had to endure

You are the bridge to my heart
That leads to the castle in my dreams
That is the dark night and the beast
That seeks to be loved and accepted
And is one third of this whole

You are the bridge to my heart
The past present and future intertwined
The selfless part that walks blind
And carries we three to our destiny
And gives us strength to be
The whole of which we three are a part.

NOVEMBER 2003

The phone rang and woke me up. I had just completed seven days on an intensive NLP course and had been chosen as one of the supportive trainers. There had been three of us helping out, and it had been a good course. I'd enjoyed every minute of it and really felt like my health and life were coming together and making sense – at last!

"Can I speak to Mr Tyler," the voice at the end of the line said.

I replied that my husband wasn't here but at work and could I take a message. She said that it was related to a sample and that they needed another one. I was none the wiser but said I would pass on the message.

My husband and I had been trying for a baby. There had been no luck for over twelve months and in many ways, I was in surrender and had prayed for guidance around this. However, it turned out that my husband took it upon himself to see a doctor, after discussing it with his friend, and have tests done. Hence, the phone call. It turned out he was infertile. In many ways, I was devastated by this news. I cried for 24 hours – in fact, I wailed! The call from the surgery felt like the final nail in the coffin of our marriage.

I just felt it was guidance and rightly or wrongly, I felt I had to leave the marriage. We discussed options over the next two weeks and saw the doctor together, but for me, in my heart it was over.

"I have to go," I said quietly and firmly. My husband looked back shocked and fearful. Tears welled up as I looked upwards. How long I had waited for this moment. "Another moment!" "Is that all life is?" an accumulation of moments that make up the essence and events of one's life.

Within a few weeks, I had found somewhere else to live and had told close family of my plans. My husband and I felt sad but also there was 'rightness' to it all. I had always felt that 2003 would be a make or break year for our marriage and so it was!

So with no job to fall back on and only my fledgling business, I left. My self-fulfilling prophesy was indeed coming true. Was it destiny or fate? I did not know for sure but it felt right. I desperately wanted to have children. I thought I was madly in love with someone else but unfortunately this was not reciprocated and even though I never left my husband for him, I did hope that it would work out.

Looking back now, I know that I ultimately left because I felt I had to follow my heart and that love would guide my path to my destiny. Seeking the answers that were still hidden from me had become more important than safety and security. Therefore, I chose to take this great risk – come what may!

As I heard Caroline Myss say two years later at her *Fate to Destiny* course that I attended: "Destiny is a high risk pursuit."

I risked it all for love and lost my beautiful three-bedroom home that we had bought together three years previously. I gave up my partner and experienced the rejection of the man I thought I was in love with! I subsequently went back to work as a nurse and took on new responsibilities like paying bills and living alone.

I faced the uncertainty of illness, my disability and aloneness, never knowing how it would work out and cried for my life, my past and the lost children. I wished my life had been different and would eventually make sense and that I would somehow come to understand it WAS all for a greater purpose and plan!

On 6th December 2003, I closed the door for the last time and never spoke with my ex-husband face to face ever again! These were his terms and I agreed to honour that request. It was nineteen years to the day since we had first met; a huge watershed in my life, and just one week before my 38th birthday.

I just prayed I was doing the right thing as I closed the door on my old life!

RESOURCES AND RECOMMENDATIONS FOR CHAPTER 4

The Love based thought system

What I see in others is a reflection of my own state of mind. I lack nothing to be happy and whole right now. My safety lies in my defencelessness, because love needs no defence. Acceptance is what brings me peace of mind. My self-worth is not based upon my performance. Love is unconditional. Forgiveness, with no exception, ensures peace. Only the present is real. The past is over and the future is not here yet.

In order for me to change my experience, I must first change my thoughts. Mistakes call for correction and learning, not judgement and punishment. I am responsible for the world I see, and I choose the feelings that I experience.

To give is to receive. For me to gain, nobody can lose. I am complete right now. My self-esteem comes from loving and accepting myself as I am today, and then sharing love and acceptance with others. I cannot change others, but I can change how I perceive others.

My self-esteem is not based upon pleasing others. I am complete, full of love and worthwhile this very instant. Healing my life begins in my mind. If I desire change, I must first look to my own mind. The past is past. The future is in the future. The present is present. Opening my heart to love makes my life full and happy. Through sharing who I am with others, I come to know who I am. I lack nothing today. Fixing you will not fix me.

Love

When Love beckons to you, follow him,
Though his ways are hard and steep,
And when his wings enfold you yield to him,
Though the sword hidden among his pinions may wound you.
And when he speaks to you believe in him,
Though his voice may shatter your dreams
as the north wind lays waste the garden

*For even as love crowns you so shall he crucify you. Even as he
is for your growth so is he for your pruning.
Even as he ascends to your height and
Caresses your tenderest branches that quiver in the sun,
So shall he descend to your roots and shake them in their cling-
ing to the earth.*

*Like sheaves of corn, he gathers you unto himself.
He threshes you to make you naked.
He sifts you to free you from your husks.
He grinds you to whiteness.
He kneads you until you are pliant;
And then he assigns you to his sacred fire, That you may become
sacred bread for God's sacred feast.*

*All these things shall love do unto you that you may know the
secrets of your heart, and in that knowledge become a fragment
of Life's heart.*

*But if in your fear you would seek only love's peace and love's
pleasure,
Then it is better for you that you cover your nakedness and pass
out of love's threshing-floor,
Into the seasonless world where you shall laugh, but not all of
your laughter, and weep, but not all of your tears.
Love gives naught but itself and takes naught but from itself.
Love possesses not nor would it be possessed;
For love is sufficient unto love.*

*When you love you should not say, "God is in my heart," but
rather, "I am in the heart of God."
And think not you can direct the course of love, for love if it
finds you worthy, directs your course.*

Love has no other desire but to fulfil itself.

*But if you love and must needs have desires, let these be your
desires:*
*To melt and be like a running brook that sings its melody to
the night.*
To know the pain of too much tenderness.
To be wounded by your own understanding of love;
And to bleed willingly and joyfully.
*To wake at dawn with a winged heart and give thanks for
another day of loving;*
To rest at the noon hour and meditate love's ecstasy;
To return home at eventide with gratitude;
*And then to sleep with a prayer for the beloved in your heart
and a song of praise upon your lips.*

KAHLIL GIBRAN (FROM THE PROPHET)

Affirmations for Unconditional Love

What you will not tell another,
You seek to hide from yourself.
What you fear another will judge,
You have already judged within yourself.
What you deny controls you.
What you withhold, imprisons you.
What you resist, drains you of Life Force.
What remains unconscious to you,
Has control over you.
What you hate you already are.
What you express, you control.
What you offer another, is no longer yours.
What you acknowledge, you are free to release.
What you embrace, empowers you.
What you yield to, you can transform.
What is in your consciousness, you can direct.
What you love, you become.

Love Manifestation Invocation

BELOVED,
The doorway is opening...
Truly, I have known you more than any other.
Your spirit overlaps mine
Like a gilt edged transparency.
It is time... I am calling,
I am calling for you from end to end,
Through all the light and shaded places throughout Creation.
What place there may be my voice cannot reach does not exist.
Beloved,
You and I have been playing hide and seek,
True Love,
Amongst the stars,
And between layers of time.
But I reveal myself and you are revealed.
It is time to return to the home,
Of each other's heart,
And to the embrace of each other's arms.
My Love, the game is over.
The sweetness and mystery of waiting,
Are no longer the food of my expectation.
I see you in the distance.
There is a haze of light about you,
Sunbeams are in your hair.
My God, the time is approaching,
My Beloved is returning,
And I am moving to you My Sweetness, Only to you...

Aaron John Beth'el in Sacred Promise Fleche's d'Amour

Books

A path with heart by Jack Kornfield

Soul Love by Sanaya Roman

The Road less travelled by M Scott Peck

Entering the Castle by Caroline Myss

Chapter 5

LET GO AND LET GOD

"Your greatness will be revealed to you at the point of destruction." – Will Smith

So often, we hope and wish for a new beginning in life, especially in any area where it has been stuck or difficult. The reason we seek out the new is that we are so darn sick of the old and yet why do we cling so long? Well, it very often is due to Karma and the fact we are not fully aware (yet!) of what has been the cause of the stuckness. Our egos find great reasons and excuses for why we are the way we are and why they should remain just so. It takes a soul with stamina and courage to blast through the old garbage and to create the right ingredients for a new beginning.

This was where I was at on 6th February 1998, as I continued my journey into the depths of my being (my dark night of the soul) that culminated in a Kundalini Awakening experience and unification with my own inner divinity!

As mentioned I had started worked with a book called *Be Your Own Counsellor* by Sheila Dainow, which I highly recommend. It is a step-by-step guide to understanding yourself better. She looks at everything from life scripts through to language patterns and ways to get to know yourself.

Although I had had counselling and various complementary therapies over the preceding ten years, it often felt like I knew more than those therapists and healers I was visiting. A very frustrating position but then again it was my life so perhaps the real issue was denial. I was on mega doses of anti-depressants at this point and was suffering from severe migraines. I had had scans and tests back in 1993 and been told I had a weakness in my right side, which may be related to one of the following; multiple sclerosis, M.E. or hemiplegic migraine. I suffered from great problems with my balance and walking was partly restricted because of this, and also, because of a lack of energy and fatigue.

When I paced myself, I could usually get by and attend to all my needs, but overall, life had become unbearable due to a relapsing/remitting cycle of improvements followed by relapses, which often left me worse than I had been, so it was a slippery slope to gradual deterioration and little in the way of improvement.

Complementary healing methods

I had turned to complementary healing methods as my doctor (although very pleasant and supportive) had little new to offer me. Since working with a holistic healer in Newburgh called Dr Melhuish and reading Louise Hays' book *You Can Heal Your Life* I knew this was my main hope of transforming my situation. I knew I could change quickly as Dr Melhuish was quite astonished when he tested my emotions with some strange device. Within four weeks, I had cleared and transformed some pretty horrible ones, including bitterness, to love and peace. He told me he had never seen anything like it. However, my body only made a slight improvement (despite changing my diet and taking numerous supplements over the years)and whilst reading *A Return to Love* by Marianne Williamson in the early Summer of 1997, a life changing event reshaped my destiny.

> *"It is in your moments of decision that your destiny is shaped."* – Anthony Robbins

My older sister, who I adored, went in for surgery for removal of an ovary. This happened at the same time as my beloved cat Tigger had to be put to sleep, as he had a tumour in his abdomen. To say I was distraught is an understatement. I loved Tigger as someone who is a parent would love their only child and we had come through some good and bad times together. He lived with my parents, as my husband had asthma and the fur irritated it somewhat. Moreover, he never really settled in our own home. Between that and my own ill health, it was agreed my parents would look after him – at least for a while!

So 21/6/97 (after being diagnosed with cancer in the spring of the same year) he was put to sleep, and oh boy did I cry!

My sister had her routine surgery that very same day too in a private hospital and all seemed well initially, but then she started to haemorrhage and ended up being rushed to the intensive care unit in Salisbury. It was touch and go for the next 48 to 72 hours, as she was ventilated and required life saving surgery to stem the blood flow. My parents drove down immediately to be at her bedside (just as well Tigger had gone, as no one would have been able to care for him that weekend). I prayed and sent healing, as I lived too far away to visit her. I was reading *Spiritual growth* by Sanaya Roman at the time too so had been practising new techniques of sending light to others and situations. Anyway, my faith in God or at least the God I was brought up to know through the church was – and had been – at an all time low for some time! My new version of God was more in alignment with *The Course in Miracles*. So I prayed and surrendered and just said: –"Don't take my sister! – I will do whatever it is you want of me in this life to the best of my ability if you let her live and be well." Thankfully, she is alive and well to this day! That summer was really the precursor to my dark night of the soul in 1998.

By March of 1998, I was taking the new medication and felt like I had a semblance of control over my body now. I did understand that by surrendering my life to God completely I was in some way invoking a new experience.

The migraines remained though and I felt the desire to heal – really heal. As much as the medication was helping, I wanted to have children with my husband and believed that I could be free of prescribed medication too. Therefore, I continued to search for better answers and solutions!

My inner world, which had always been rich and intense continued to throw up new material and synchronicities. I remember watching *Tess of The D'Urbervilles,* which was being shown on BBC Television and then I dreamt about Michael. The first time I had for a while. Even with all the letting go and shift it was almost as if I could not break free from the past. I felt like I was on a treadmill and nothing seemed to be able to completely break the pattern despite all the inner work, journalling and releasing I was doing in 1998.

I worked on my life script related to the work of Eric Berne and recorded my answers.

You might want to give it a go too.

12/3/98
This is what I wrote about my script back then:

Triumph over Despair

A fast moving story with many twists and turns; tragic in many ways, but ultimately hopeful and triumphant. Me and two men – making choices.

A happy ending!

By the middle of April 1998, I was back at square one (or so it seemed).

I wrote two pieces that described my despair that anything was ever going to change. Thick gluey depression enveloped me as I fought my inner demons and went through the climax of my dark night of my soul on one especially difficult Saturday evening!

25/4/98

The End

When is the end?
Is it soon?
Or am I
Crawling along towards a slow death

Hand over fist
Trying to keep going
For what?

When is the end?
Will I know that it's time
Or will it sneak up on me
And take me abruptly
Quickly, spontaneously!

When is the end
I scream aloud
How much longer to sustain this pointless existence?
Unmeasurable pity
Loss of dignity
And the final irony
When is the end?
Will I embrace it joyfully
Or limp towards it fearfully?

I wrote *Untitled* as I wrestled with suicide. The curtain pole and the image of me hanging from it became very appealing that night and it is the closest I have ever been to ending my life as I truly had, had ENOUGH! Sandy was working very late and I just felt so alone with all of my troubles!

Untitled

Will I make it through the night
Or be found dead at first light
Empty and spent
Tired of this circus
Broken down and bent

Today is such a long day
So many long days I have now spent
Alone and apart from the Human race

Passing the time – for what?
An endless, pointless journey
Devoid of all meaning
At long last
Is all I am saying

Incoherent is how I feel
Senseless, pointless hopeless
Despair so deep I cannot tell
Where it ends and I begin
I just know it's ever there
Ever present, ever draining

So low I sink
Unable to find the link
That has brought me to this point
I just know I can never think
Of joy and happiness
Ever ever again!

Well I made it through that part of my dark night and surrendered my life to God once more – I let go and let God take over.

Things changed again that very next day. I went to meet my new friend Wendy Brandie in Tayport, and she was the catalyst for my next big shift. She gave me The Dalai Lama's autobiography and also recommended a cranio-sacral therapist. This would lead me to let go and let God, fully igniting my Kundalini Awakening experience.

I wrote this on the 5th May 1998

May Dawn

So here I am, still limping
Slowly along, grasping at straws
Looking for any light, to guide my path
A new month has dawned

Warmer and brighter
Bringing each new day
Closer to the summer

Is it enough to keep me alive?
Or will it not stop me from the dive
Into despair and darkest snare
Of this lonely, tiresome existence
Getting through each day is too long
So I take it one hour at a time
My mind pacing up and down
Planning escape, pounding at the high perimeter fence
Looking for any weakness
In my captors' defence

Such a strange life I live
Like a chameleon, always showing
Another face to those around me
While inside I grieve and mourn
For all my youthful years gone past
Reflecting on what might have been
Had I not succumbed to the evil cast
By an invisible intruder
That ties me down and lays me bare
Begging for mercy, pleading my case
All I have left is hope I swear

Meeting Beth

On the 19th May 1998, I went to see Beth Benton. She was from Houston in Texas and had moved to Newburgh in Fife a few years previously. Apparently, she was on her way to Germany and had stopped off in Scotland for a week or so. She loved it so much she just stayed, and set up her business in Fife allowing our paths to cross. She would be the one that would help me really get my body out of its stuck place.

I remember as I was being taken to see her in the car that my inner voice was saying "this is it" and somehow I knew I was ready to clear something big (like the last ten years!) Beth was both a psychologist and a cranio-sacral therapist/body worker, so she knew her stuff. When I arrived at her flat, the first obstacle was getting up to the fourth floor.

As I couldn't walk up anymore than one flight of stairs without fear of a relapse, my husband had to carry me up the stairs. That alone was a big incentive to shift my life. I was tired of being dependent and having a body that had no energy. Beth asked me lots of questions and I answered them honestly.

"You have no energy?" she asked.

"Yes, that's right," I said, "just like there's a blockage and I only have so much for every day, which doesn't fill me up like it once did!"

I wrote this after that first meeting.

Words

Words can never describe
The way I feel tonight
So drained and stripped of life
Dead inside and without fight I lie here silent and sore
Unable to speak or give voice
To these terrible feelings inside

So deep is this despair
That nothing can ever compare
With the isolation and fear
I live with daily, unable to care
For myself or my hopes anymore
No choice, no life, no future
Only bitter recriminations and painful sighs
Emerge from me tonight

Like a tree dead to the core
My fruit and leaves decayed and laid bare

Already past its best
Only fit for the woodcutters pile
No longer growing and flourishing
Every day as I should
Instead I wait with a tired heart
For some resolution or end to this life

On the second meeting with Beth, 26th May 1998 (just as the new Moon lit up my north node – which is related to my life purpose), I just poured everything out. I told her about my experience in Corfu, my marriage, my health problems, my interest in astrology and my family history.

It felt like a confession and in retrospect, it was just that – a fifth chakra release of my past and the calling back of my spirit into my body!

After I emptied my heart and soul to her, she had me lie up on her treatment table and she did some bodywork. Returning to my seat, she simply told me that she thought I was a very special gifted person. That alone amazed me, as I really felt so low and despondent about my life!

I went home that night and felt lighter than I had for years!

I wrote *Release* to mark this shift.

Release

Freedom is what I seek
Freedom from these invisible chains
That tie me so tightly to the past
When I was that other person

Time to release the past
And walk forward, fears outcast
Letting go of all the pain
Seems so hard to do
I've held it so long that
I know not where it ends and I begin

Gingerly I lie back
Close my eyes and relax
Let go and release at last
No need to hold on so tightly
To my fears, tears and despair
Time to let go of shadows and dreams
Glimpses of a better future beckon

I breathe in deeply
Take all my courage in both hands
And slowly start to release
Inch by inch
Breath after breath
Freedom at last
Permission to let go of my past!

On the 28th May (as described at the start of chapter 1) I was guided to buy *Why People Don't Heal and How They Can* by Caroline Myss at the book shop and thus my spiritual awakening experience was now in full flow! I wrote in my journal: "Everything is coming together and starting to make sense (at last!)."

Suddenly so many things that had been happening began to fall into place. I prayed and asked for forgiveness for myself and forgave those I needed to.

The next day I relapsed and felt like I was back to square one – again!

I wrote this inner dialogue on 31st May 1998.

Dedicated to my 12th house

Oh how can I appease thee
Great fate and ruler of my destiny
When will I make you see
That I am ready to be set free

Archaic ruler of my deep soul I've kept you locked up and
without air
For so long, you have been hidden there
Repressed and stunted with time
Until you planned this great revenge
And took my life and laid me bare
Screaming for light, you did not care
This is how it feels, you yelled
To be locked up year after year

Now I gently caress you
And whisper my forgiveness, while I plead for mercy
Be my friend and let us join united at last
Neither black nor white
But merged and imperfect
To stand together as One
Oh Moon, Pluto Uranus
How great thou art
And how small am I
Without you in my life
I can never be all that you demand of me!

The next day I was unwell and yet I had heightened sense of clarity and awareness. I was guided to listen to *The Gateless Gate* By Dick Sutphen – a guided three dimensional journey that takes you into an imaginary retreat where you play the central character. I had listened to it a few times before, but this time something BIG shifted!

I had a satori experience and came back from it a different person.

Suddenly I was transcending the pain and fatigue and, even though I was still ill at that moment and in a relapse, I was in level ten of the enlightenment process (see Chapter 1 – Neptunian states) and my heart was wide open! I was able to transcend my own desires and love from the divine source within me. My personal Will and divine Will merged and my throat chakra opened, allowing me to heal – really heal as I let go and let God take over!

RESOURCES AND RECOMMENDATIONS FOR CHAPTER 5

Saturn is the cosmic schoolteacher and rules the ego in astrology. It is also the ruler of Capricorn, the sign of the goat climbing to the mountaintop and being ready for the next initiation. It is often called *the doorway into spirit* and is the sign associated with fulfilment of ambitions and the destiny point (midheaven). In a spiritual sense, this means aligning the lower self with the higher self and allowing your soul's purpose to manifest through the integration of your dual nature i.e. becoming more balanced such that your ONENESS and at one-ment with the higher Christ, self manifests.

Some questions to reflect on as you let go and let God:

a. Are you living the life you know you were born to live? If not, then why not?

b. Do you feel the structures and forms in your life support you?

c. How aware are you of your role in the Universe that only YOU have been born to fulfil?

d. Does your reality reflect your spiritual beliefs e.g. Are you living in abundance consciousness and trust or coming from lack or fear?

e. Do you know/trust that you can manifest everything you require to live your life purpose?

The Saboteur: Your Guardian of Choice transforms into the Magician

The saboteur is the Archetype of illusion. The saboteur sees the illusions, all of the reasons – notice this is the Archetype of reasons, of rationale – all the reasons why it will not work. Why you cannot do what you are here to do is based on illusions, and it is governed by the illusion. The Magician is the Master of illusion. It can see through the illusions, it can see through the chaos and see the balance. You know you have a sacred purpose and it is inside of YOU ready to unfold when YOU action it!

Some questions to move out of sabotage

Ask yourself the following:

☞ What reasons and excuses do you give yourself about your inaction?

☞ Identify what would change if you became more empowered.

☞ What do you need to give up (secondary gains) to live a more authentic life?

☞ Now look at how your life would be if you started to be the real you!

☞ How do you sabotage others?

☞ What are you presently sabotaging in your life? What's the truth coming up about yourself that you don't want to see that required this situation? What is it that you are battling? If there's another person involved, you cannot mention that person's name from this point on.

Recommended books

Saturn – A New Look at an Old Devil by Liz Greene

The Hope by Andrew Harvey

Why People Don't Heal and How They Can by Caroline Myss

Chapter 6

TELL THE TRUTH

"Our deepest fear is not that we are inadequate. Our deepest fear is that we are powerful beyond measure. It is our light, not our darkness that most frightens us. We ask ourselves, who am I to be brilliant, gorgeous, talented, fabulous? Actually, who are you not to be? You are a child of God. Your playing small does not serve the world. There is nothing enlightened about shrinking so that other people won't feel insecure around you. We are all meant to shine, as children do. We were born to make manifest the glory of God that is within us. It's not just in some of us; it's in everyone. And as we let our own light shine, we unconsciously give other people permission to do the same. As we are liberated from our own fear, our presence automatically liberates others." Marianne Williamson

A subject very close to my own heart is how to make friends and work with your shadow. We all have one, and it is often the repository of many positive life-enhancing qualities, as well as those ones we feel unable to express.

Sometimes it is quite inappropriate for us to express certain qualities, while at other times we may shock people when we do!

Carl Jung first coined the phrase and most of us view it rather negatively or at least with some trepidation. It takes much courage to explore it and begin to acknowledge and own parts of ourselves that may have been kept well in check or even completely repressed.

One definition might be that it is the dark, unlit and repressed side of the ego complex. However, it mainly accounts for all that is within you that is unknown to you. To complicate matters, you may be connected with the shadow of the collective unconscious, and this means that you not only have your own personal stuff to uncover, but also much that rages in the planetary airwaves to contend with.

In working with unlocking your sacred purpose, the shadow will be an important aspect to gain insight and dialogue with. Bringing contents from the unconscious realm up to conscious awareness takes time and can be a slow painstaking process, until we become more skilled.

Ultimately, the more of your shadow that is hidden the more it will wreak havoc on your personal energy and health. It takes a lot of energy to keep it held in check and often on first examination, it is easier to stuff it back in the closet and pray it does not show up again – at least in this lifetime.

So having a guide or spiritual coach can help in looking at how it is affecting you and ways to allow it gradually to become visible, socialised, transformed and accepted as part of who you are.

Carl Jung once said, *"Until you make the unconscious conscious, it will direct your life and you will call it fate."*

This was where I was in June 1998. I had had my satori moment and was in the midst of truly dissolving the old me, but as yet, had not birthed the new one!

As Jack Kornfield states in his book *A Path With Heart* – *"When we can finally look at the horrors and joys, our birth and our death, the gain and loss of all things, with an equal heart and open mind, there arises the state of the most beautiful and profound equanimity."*

I knew something profound was occurring to me, and my heightened mood and senses were in no way aligned with my physical body, which was still weak and powerless. I just knew something within that was indestructible was now accessible – it was the divine part of me and I could feel it. All the fears were gone and I was almost euphoric with the sense of wonderment at it!

I had released all attachment, leaving me at peace with God, and myself.

"The soul that is attached to anything, however much good there may be in it, will not arrive at the liberty of The Divine," said St John of The Cross. At that moment – I knew that to be – oh so true!

We all go through cycles of death and rebirth of course during our lifetime, just like the caterpillar that retreats into its cocoon, unsure of what will emerge and facing its own demise before it is reborn as the beautiful – yet unknown new form – a butterfly.

> *"Mystical flight inevitably follows your cocoon experience.*
> *The ego dies in the cocoon so that the soul can take flight."*
> C Myss *5th Mansion of Entering The Castle – Dissolving*
> *into Holiness – From Silkworm to Butterfly*

At this point, in May 1998, I was breaking out of the chrysalis that had held me for over a year and was held in this space of waiting with such reverence that I can even feel the memory of it as I write.

As Jack Kornfield describes in his aforementioned book, I had been in a very dark night of my soul indeed! Even though I had surrendered and been following the guiding light of my soul for months, I still had to face my demons and release myself from my past fully to be reborn. And even though freedom and liberation from it had become most important to me, Kornfield describes how we still hit the impossible place where we cannot let go any further.

This is the stage of great doubt where we can become restless, the world is too difficult and I had indeed wished I could quit and go home to my bed or God (my feelings of suicide in April 1998) or my Mother and feel safe as the poems and prose I had written in my journal show. This last moment of great doubt seemed to be the immediate experience before the satori moment and subsequent awakening to my *I Am presence within*!

Now that I was through it, I was held in this wonderful space of high equanimity. This is where consciousness is fully open and awake, perfectly balanced. This is a level of wonderful peace and I wrote *Awakening* on 2/6/98 whilst I was in that space.

2/6/98

Awakening

Today I opened my eyes
And at long last
I could see reality
So long I have slept
In the turbulent waters
Of my worst nightmares
Unable to wake or see any light
I tossed and turned
Fear after fear building up, year after year
Inside of me

And now I know
I will never close my eyes again
For I have faced my monster
In the dead of night
And slayed it for once and all
Never again will I sleep
The long sleep of the dead
Or the drunk
Or the unconscious
For I have been awakened
Forever!

Great joy cleanses every vein and artery
As I wake
Refreshed
Rejuvenated
Revitalised

Ready to take on any new task
And become that which I have denied
For many a long year
YIPEE!

Exploring Your Secret Self

So facing our shadow and experiencing the dark night of the soul (should we have to) is a huge subject of course.

Without owning the shadow or the wisdom that we are all one i.e. all connected on this planet – we project our negativity, fears and anxieties onto the nearest scapegoat(s) who looks either weak or strong enough to carry these energies and issues. This is how we end up with marginalised groups, wars, Nazis, holocausts, fascism and global warming. Not a pretty result.

So my hope is that by accepting you have one and being willing to delve into exploring yours, it may help the planet heal and your friends and family come to know more of the 'real' you. Moreover, it may be keeping your sacred purpose well and truly locked up and without air, so this is even more reason to get in tune with yourself in this area. We have 'banned the shadow' as a culture and often look the other way!

What happens when we do that?

Let's explore it and discover more about your shadow, my shadow and the collective shadow that keeps us trapped in lower vibrations.

It is so true that we all want to feel good and happy, which is perfectly understandable and yet if we neither care nor challenge many of society's less than savoury actions against minority groups and classes, then we are all doomed!

Yes, I say this and yet surely, as we are all closer to enlightenment, we should know better. We do, of course, at an intellectual level and we can spot this happening to us and around us. However, it is much easier to say it is someone else's problem rather than address our side of the challenge.

A lot of the media and TV support these viewpoints and, like it or not, we are all heavily influenced by the images consciously or unconsciously. The media talks of underdogs, victims, victors and champions. It loves to project good and bad views depending on what is the flavour of the day. Jade Goody is a great example of someone who not only suffered from shadow energies but also was part of the collective who inflicted them. Remember *Big Brother* and Shilpa Shetty on racism! These are all examples we see played out in front of us and we all complain when we are affected or being victimised personally, whether it's by the housebuyers trying to pull a fast one, the banks who refuse us money for our business, or our boss not putting us forward for promotion!

So where does this all lead us? Well it means we have to be alert to the fact that as we work at deeper levels of awakening, new material will emerge from the unconscious. This can cause great stirrings and pain when we realise what we have been doing or being. As Carl Jung said, "There is no coming to consciousness without pain."

Kahlil Gibran in *The Prophet* states: *"Much of your pain is self-chosen. It is the bitter potion by which the physician within you heals your sick self."*

Pain and working with shadow energies are intertwined cosmic bedfellows. We have to learn to address our individual shadow first, and then look at it in the groups we are each involved in, for the sake of ourselves, our families and our communities or we will continue to create a world of divisions and violence.

Tribal energies and being part of a group is very supportive for us all. In fact, it is essential to feel part of a community and group or we then face isolation and loss of this belonging. So what happens when that group wants you as an individual to play by its rules? Well, you can either work to influence the group by making something a win–win situation for all, or you can risk getting kicked out of it if that doesn't work. You can choose to leave of your own accord or lastly, you may just capitulate and remain silent playing out the victim role until you do! Then you risk feeling inferior and lost until you have the strength to walk away or address the issues/bullying that is occurring. Of course, you have to own that you have projected your fears onto the group and vice versa, but only in a context of forgiveness, reconciliation, understanding and accommodating differences can this ever occur. Discussion and being open to both the challenge and the transformation is both healing and dynamic.

This led me to explore my secret self. As mentioned, I read a book of the same title back in 1990, just as my health problems were escalating into what would become full blown M.E. I remember going to buy the book as it was all about the 12th house in astrology and the most hidden part of the chart.

At the personal level, we each have a gift to receive through the shadow work we embark upon!

Transformation requires awareness and astrology is the 'crème de la crème' in bringing awareness and shining a light on your blind spots.

It gave me the opportunity for self-discovery and gradually helped with the recovery of 'parts' of my shadow, thus transforming my fate (feeling powerless) and myself, moving towards my destiny (empowerment)!

By facing deep-seated fears, we become aware of latent abilities, talents, inner strengths and gifts that may have been trapped deep in the recesses of our mind and soul – in our shadow!

Joseph Campbell said, *"The treasure you seek is in the cave you fear to enter."*

Birthing the True you!

"A journey of a thousand miles begins with the first step." The Tao

So how do you birth the REAL YOU?

A song by one of my favourite bands is called *The Birth of the True* and one day I was listening to the *Greatest Hits* by Aztek Camera, led by the inimitable Roddy Frame, when I had this insight!

I first heard of the band in the early 1980s when I was outside sunbathing and heard a neighbour blasting them from an upstairs window. Funny how things 'start' in life.

A bit like love affairs, new friendships and career changes; suddenly we are aware of 'something' new that we immediately are drawn to.

As Liz Greene describes in her classic book *The Astrology of Fate*; this is how it started – but what is this? She describes how Dr Gerard Adler met a Mrs Adler – same name! – at a party who, over a short period of time, introduced him to the ideas of Carl Jung and synchronicity. Chance, fate, nurturing an inner preparedness for change and direction. The fate of two people was deeply intertwined in a complex pattern because of what in ordinary language, one can only call a 'chance meeting'. Here we discern a 'meaningful coincidence' – the same name and then a mutual interest that changes one's life. He went on to write *Reflections on Chance, Fate and Synchronicity* and by virtue of this meeting with Mrs Adler, met and worked with Carl Jung.

My own synchronicity occurred as I thought of writing about this topic and alerted me to listen to the song that was playing and something told me – it was meaningful to the moment. So I paid attention and here is the insights I received, based on the song of the same name – *birth of the true!*

At the time I first heard of Aztek Camera, they were pretty much unknown and coming from Westwood East Kilbride myself, perhaps that neighbour and I were their first fans – viral marketing at its most simplistic level! I certainly enjoyed what I heard that day and went out and bought their debut album *High Land Hard Rain*, which was released in April 1983.

The album was successful gathering significant critical acclaim for its well crafted, multilayered pop.

The band went on to release a total of six albums, although most of these were essentially written and played by Frame pretty quickly. Thus, my love affair with Aztek Camera began and their songs gave my own life some meaning and purpose over the years!

Partly that is due to the lyrics, which always seemed to resonate with a lot of my own thoughts and feelings, even in my teenage years – values like truth, hope, optimism and *joie de vivre* – along with the realisation that life can be pretty rubbish for many people.

The title is all about birthing the true and that in itself means letting go of illusions, pretence, fears and anything that masks what we stand for. When we truly birth ourselves in the truth, or what is true for us, we have to let go and trust that what we meet will reflect our new state. Whilst we live in anything less than that we risk being drawn into power games, secret agendas and a life that will ultimately fall short of something very valuable – integrity and love.

Of course, it can take many years for us to want to live from the core of our being and understand what truth means for each of us. There may be no absolute truth but there certainly is a field that we enter that is all about purity of word, thought and action – that for me is the truth and from there we live a life that will support the best of everything this world can offer. Not especially easy, however, when we look around and listen to the news of propaganda, deceit, illusion and greed.

I guess even as a teenager I just knew that one day I would get to this space and want to know and live my truth, my life purpose and be free of others' lies, projections, approval and expectations.

Here's to Roddy Frame and You – the birth of the true You!

Truth is not contingent upon one's belief in it, altered by the words one chooses to describe it or wounded if neglected. It is simply TRUTH!

RESOURCES AND RECOMMENDATIONS FOR CHAPTER 6

So, in working with the shadow, here are a few tips and quotes to help heal the pain within:

Astrology can help you understand much more about your life and purpose than years of psychotherapy, NLP, coaching and hypnosis, together might ever fully uncover. To utilise the knowledge of astrology alongside these mediums is like a laser focussing on exactly what is going on NOW and what you need to pay attention to or work with and transform.

Your astrology chart is THE quintessential treasure map of YOU!

The houses in your chart are like the playground, so knowing your time of birth is essential to capture what planets (your Archetypes) are playing their roles out in. One house that is much maligned and misunderstood even by astrologers, is the 12th House. This is the most hidden part of your chart and relates to your unconscious processes. I like to think of it as the house of 'grace', as it is where we have least control and yet can experience the miraculous through surrender to a higher power. If you have planets in your 12th house, find that you are very sensitive and often feel misunderstood, then an exploration of them may help here.

First, some keywords for the 12th house are:

Spirituality, achilles heel, burdens we carry, family and/or collective Karma, shame, guilt, past lives, hidden resources, escapism, dreams, repressions, all or nothing behaviour, illness, psychosomatic illnesses, hospitals and prison, what is hidden from society, scapegoats, seclusion, victim/martyr tendencies, secret fantasies, unfinished business, genius, inspiration, volunteer work, service, gifts and talents, sacrifices, secrets, mixed messages, purpose and mission, confinement, gremlin, solitude, transcendence, spiritual devotion and selfless love, saints, secret enemies, self-defeating behaviours, and service to the 'whole'.

It is often associated with people who work in the fields of caring (hospitals and prisons) or who are incarcerated due to 'bad behaviours' – sometimes for their own good, and sometimes to protect society from their complex and harmful outbursts.

So we see the wide spectrum from Joan of Arc (Neptune in her 12th house) to Adolf Hitler (Uranus), who have planets in the 12th house!

As you can see, we need to look at each planet that resides there to gauge how it may be acting out its role.

With Joan of Arc who eventually died for a cause and her belief in God, we see Neptune. Neptune is all about transcending the trials of earthly life and being aligned with divine love. It is also the natural ruler of the 12th house, so it is at 'home' there.

The 12th house is very much associated with having a 'calling' and for those who have planets there it is almost certainly something they will have to pursue or they will never feel 'whole'. It is the house that brings us to wholeness and without an examination and integration of our Archetypes in it, we may walk around feeling we are 'missing' something or someone.

Mainly we need to connect to source to fill the 'hole' or else we will end up in a place of abandonment and feel rejected by society – often a scapegoat – or deemed to be a troublemaker (another role that can be played out). Van Gogh and Oscar Wilde had planets in their 12th house and they both exhibited many of the aforementioned traits.

It is often the house of genius but there is a thin line between genius and madness.

Many people with full or complex 12th houses ended up in ashrams (nuns, monks, priests, etc.) in the past or had mental illnesses that caused suicidal feelings, as they just 'didn't fit in' to society. Their sensitivity often led them to breaking point and surrendering to a greater power (light) or the taking of their own life (shadow). Nowadays it can still be problematic but you are more likely to see these people being of service through selfless service or affiliated to much of the 'new age' practices, as the collective shadow is brought to the surface.

Adolf Hitler had Uranus here, which is all about sudden revolutionary change and independent thought that is connected with collective ideology. He was a mouthpiece for what was in the 'air' in the 1930s – so although he is seen to be 'evil' by many, he simply led the way in expressing the ideology of Nazism – which is why it is too easy to blame one person for all the ills of any time! We are connected. We are all ONE and until we each examine our shadows and understand what is truly happening at these deep levels, then we are often just projecting the blame and seeing it mirrored through another or society.

In astrological terms, the shadow is also somewhat related to the planet Pluto and the sign of Scorpio. Pluto is the deity that is invisible and lives in the underworld. Similar to the myth of Persephone, often it can feel like you have been abducted when Pluto makes significant aspects to your birth chart and you may feel forced to face the demons and darkness that have been avoided until this time.

We all have light and shadow within us and the dark shadow can cause unacceptable behaviours. As we are all connected to one another, it is clear that as we heal darkness within ourselves, we redeem and liberate humanity too.

Some people carry not only personal energies but also transpersonal patterns, and this can be seen as a Karmic burden or as a gift! At the soul level, you may have agreed to carry these for those who are not able to acknowledge it (yet!), or as a learning process, to love unconditionally (to be a vessel for God or a channel for peace) and not harm others in any way regardless of how they may treat you. So it is related to both your Karma and your dharma!

Pluto is the smallest of all the planets but paradoxically seen as the most powerful in astrological terms. It rules the sign of Scorpio in western astrology and Pisces in esoteric astrology. It is linked to the collective unconscious and power issues that are impersonal or appear bigger than our ego self!

Discovered in the early 1930s it was synchronised with the rise of fascism and Nazi idealism.

Pluto means 'riches' and is the Lord of the Underworld, and was originally called Hades.

It rules power, fate and to some extent, the necessity to face up to and transform your Karmic lot into the gift and blessing it can be! Thus, you become empowered as you navigate your shadow.

Pluto in your birth chart can show where you have the tendency to give your power away – be it to God, your job, your partner or your beliefs around money or happiness.

Wherever it is transiting can show what area you are working on right now and how to navigate this more easily with grace and understanding. Always by excavating your shadow, you will meet these issues and learn more about how powerful you truly are!

> *"Pluto is the giver of wholeness, a storehouse of abundant riches, a place not of fixation in torment but a place if propitiated rightly that offers fertile plenty."* – James Hillman

Books

Entering the Castle – An Inner Path to God and Your Soul by Caroline Myss

Towards Mystical Union by Julienne McLean

Healing Pluto Problems by Donna Cunningham

The Astrology of Fate by Liz Greene

Quotes

☞ In a time of Universal deceit, truth-telling becomes a revolutionary act. – George Orwell

☞ Truth is a matching grant – to the extent that you can afford to see it is the extent it is given to you – C Myss

☞ Recognise that shadow energies appear when it's time to resolve and integrate them.

☞ Feeling blocked is a sure sign that you are needing to forgive or do release work.

☞ Inner work is essential or else you will continue to blindly project onto others what pain you have that is unresolved.

☞ Dialogue and support with a spiritual director or coach can help here.

☞ Be clear with those who are offending you where your boundaries are and ask them to respect these and vice versa.

☞ Move away from bullying until it subsides or the energies are transmuted.

☞ Ask yourself what wants me?

☞ Forgive, forgive, forgive.

☞ Love hearts and stop judging.

☞ You must live what you believe or change your beliefs to create inner peace and harmony.

☞ Love the good and the bad and the ugly – when you can do this with an open heart and a non-judgemental mind, then you will be truly beautiful and the God or Goddess that is within will shine forth like a diamond.

Chapter 7

SEEK AND YE SHALL FIND

*"Each person comes into this world with a specific destiny –
she has something to fulfil, some message has to be delivered,
some work has to be completed. You are not here accidentally
– you are here meaningfully. There is a purpose behind you.
The whole intends to do something through you."* – Osho

There has certainly been a lot of seeking in my life. Having my Sun in Sagittarius with the key words 'I seek', that is not really that surprising to me.

The seeker Archetype goes in search of knowledge and wisdom with a degree of curiosity. The shadow seeker can take one down blind alleyways leading to an aimless and pointless journey with no resolution!

For me, the journey had taken me through many spiritual experiences, culminating in a Kundalini Awakening in June 1998.

After my satori moment and writing *Awakening*, I continued to read *Why People Don't Heal and How They Can*. I recognised myself in one particularly rich passage and it felt like the key that unlocked Aladdin's cave for me. This was where all my riches were stored.

In this passage, Caroline talks about symbolic reasoning, and how we all have a victim with us. This is the part of us that we meet in situations that disempower us, just as my panic attacks and anxiety/depression had done so, in my early teens. Throughout my twenties and thirties I was disempowered by M.E., alongside my obsessive love for Michael, and finally facing up to my own death through suicide in 1998 – having never become empowered enough to solve the mystery of my life. This had taken me to complete surrender point.

Suddenly lights were coming on and I knew that this illness was my bugaboo that I was ready to confront and face no matter what!

I sang the song from *Titanic* by Celine Dion – and wept again as I got to the lines: "You're here there's NOTHING I fear. You are safe in my heart and my heart will go on and on." Just as I had cried in February and let go of Michael, I now knew that he had been my saving grace and helped me face my fears. Just as Jack had 'saved' Rose in Titanic, so my mystical experience of divine love had taken me to the very core of my being safe at last!

In the book *Man's Search For Meaning*, Victor Frankl explains how those who had a 'dream' survived the horrendous 'reality' of Auschwitz – those who didn't, died – and my dream that somehow I would see Michael again and marry him had kept me alive at my darkest moments. Even screaming out his name at these times had probably called Archangel Michael to me (albeit unknowingly) – the great protector of mankind.

Victor Frankl discovered that the number one reason people died was because they gave up hope. Every day, he helplessly witnessed friends being escorted to the death chambers, and yet he trumped fate by deciding his own destiny. Frankl realised that his internal perception could not be taken away by anyone or anything outside of himself. He knew that *they* could not affect *his* internal mindset. Hope lived in his heart despite the fact that he was surrounded by such horrific circumstances.

Frankl went on to say, *"Everyone has his own specific vocation or mission in life to carry out a concrete assignment, which demands fulfillment. Therein he cannot be replaced, nor can his life be repeated. Thus, everyone's task is as unique as his specific opportunity to implement it."* This wisdom tells us that our most important job is to find our 'real work' and do it with all our heart. Frankl's will to find meaning kept him alive. Holding on to hope gave him a personal sense of empowerment that allowed him to make it through. Eventually he was released and went on to give us the gift of Logo therapy, which helps people find the meaning in their lives. His is a prime example of how our unique destiny gives meaning to our existence and has a bearing on our creative work.

This chimed in perfectly with my own journey from darkness into the light in 1998.

I wrote *No going back* on 3/6/98 in this high state of high equanimity.

3/6/98

No going back

You can never go back
Once you have penetrated the mist
And seen the scorching light
Of another world
Just as real as this one
Less tangible at times
But still available
If you only take the time
To close your eyes and listen
First to your heartbeat
And then in the distance
A drum, which beats a new rhythm
In time with your breath
All encompassing and revealing
A new direction beckons
No more dead ends
No more tears

No more fears
Once you tune into this beat
You can never go back
And forget what you have
Stumbled upon
Everything is illumined in a flash
A single ray of insight
Is all that it takes to start
And then you know with certainty
You can never go back
The line is drawn
Tomorrow's world has begun!

I then watched a film called *Photographing Fairies*, which is all about seeing through illusions.

The next day I saw Beth and told her about my expansive state and how everything was going to be just fine. She was certainly pleased for me but she asked me if I had had any direct guidance about physical healing. I said that I felt I needed to come off the medications I was on, as they may have been toxic, and take a new mineral formula, which had shown up through a healing centre I was being treated by. This cheered her up. So next, I was on her treatment couch and a significant emotional event that had happened when I was at primary school came up for me.

It had been near to the break and as children do, I was just wishing it would come so that I could go to the loo! Anyway, the teacher had decided to choose who was to play different parts for her upcoming play. She wanted me to audition for the part of narrator. I remember feeling confused. I seem to remember that I knew I needed to go the loo as my bladder was about to burst but somehow embarrassed and feeling out of control, I just did as she asked and stood up in front of the whole class to audition. Of course, I couldn't stop myself, and next thing I knew I had wet myself. It was probably the most humiliating experience of my life! It left me feeling deeply ashamed and distraught. The panic attacks later on partly stemmed from that event and my fear of feeling so humiliated and out of control ever again. This caused me to lack trust in myself and surrendering to God became my biggest fear. As it came up for me on the treatment couch, it felt like a thick plug of ancient mucus was released by Beth. I cried and felt the pain I had blocked for so many years release – at last!

This was the next major turning point for me and the next day I had my kundalini experience.

4 JUNE 1998

The Kundalini Awakening experience

After I returned from Beth's on the 4th June 1998, I felt empowered, renewed and so excited!

I couldn't sleep all night and had the feeling that I was flying. I remember singing *I believe I can fly* by R Kelly, and I was in such an expanded state of consciousness. Around 5 a.m., I got up and told my husband who was sleeping next door about this joy. He laughed and said, "Well you'll be tired with no sleep." But I wasn't! I started to feel ecstatic waves of energy go through my spine as I breathed deeply, and suddenly I was having what is termed a 'Kundalini Awakening'.

I wrote this at 5.30 a.m. that same day:

Peaceful

Relaxed and able to let go at last
Deep rejuvenating sleep
From which I wake
Renewed and revitalised
Filled with spiritual joy
So pure it sparkles in my eyes
The fears of yesterday outcast
As I gently heal my physical body
Which has endured so much on my behalf
Thank you body for your strength
Now I treat you with new respect
All the ingredients that you need

Sleep
Healthy diet
Cleansing
Exercise
Love

I bow to your higher knowledge
For you have known all along
What the problem was
You spoke but I did not hear
You cried but still I did not hear
You screamed but still I did not hear
And then you crumbled
And boy did I know all about it
But still I would not listen
Until now and I will never stop listening
I promise!

Over the next two days, I was able to heal my body and walk further than I had for years! I held new insights and had a new awareness around my life purpose, and how to live from this new perspective. I felt like a master – a master of my life and destiny – at last!

I wrote this on the 7th June 1998

Grounded

Coming down to Earth
Slowly but sure
Feeling calm and at peace
Released and free
Still bound to the divine plan
But now I play the starring role
I always knew was for me

Great thanks and prayers
I send to the force

For all the lives I have spent
Working towards this one
Of revelation and enlightenment
My faith and trust held firm
And delivered me into this new day

Now I know I am on the path
Upward but still rooted
In planet Earth
I pledge my life to care for
My fellow man to help him
To realise this feeling
Of love joy and forgiveness

Guided as always by God
I listen for each cue
Patient and trusting
Knowing I am safe
Now and for always
All the way to eternity

So I was in the Enlightenment State

The 11th and final state is where mystical experiences or cosmic consciousness takes over and your boundaries completely drop as your ego merges with spirit and you receive an influx of healing and rejuvenating cosmic energy. It lasted a few hours, maybe even days, but the impact and transformational experience stayed with me forever and the memory of it has helped to guide me ever since!

JUNE 2008

Going from what if to what is

It was now time to go from what ifs to what is! In an attempt to see the perfection of your mission, I recommend keeping a journal. Writing your way to freedom and joy can really shine a light on your mission and soul's purpose!

That is where I was when I decided to write this book and share my own journey. I attended a writing workshop in June 2008. It was to be a time of turning points and seeking for answers to my many questions and what felt like unfinished business.

I had lost my Dad on the 7th May 2008. He passed on quite suddenly and unexpectedly from chronic renal failure related to nephritis. The condition was diagnosed the previous autumn, and the experimental treatment comprising of steroids and chemotherapy was unsuccessful. It had actually put him into a weakened state and at risk of succumbing to infections. He had been in and out of hospital for weeks and eventually he passed on peacefully in the early hours of Wednesday morning, the 7th May 2008. Again, it was Mary (my Dad's real mother), who seemed to be around me on the days leading up to his death. I remember watching a concert on TV that Saturday evening the 3rd May and hearing *Let it Be* – it felt as if it was sign of the events that would unfold.

The next day the doctor told us they did not expect him to recover, as my dad was now in a coma from which he never regained full consciousness.

My Dad's background

My Dad was born on the 6th October 1940, and at birth, his name was John Mclean. His parents Johnny McLean and Mary McLean (nee Potter) were in the midst of World War Two when Mary became unwell with childbirth fever quite quickly after my Dad's birth. She passed on six weeks later, November 19th 1940, just two weeks short of her 21st birthday! Due to there being no antibiotics, she died a fairly common death for women of child-bearing years – hard to believe now but true.

My Dad was then cared for by his grandmother (Mary's mother), as his father had to go to Algeria, and by the time he was five, he had been adopted by his gran and his name was changed to John Mclean Potter.

My Dad was an only child but he had lots of half brothers now and cousins who all mucked in to care for him. He was fairly insecure though, and

I believe the loss of his mother at such a young age was almost certainly a contributory factor. His father went on to re-marry and have three more children, so my Dad had two half-sisters and one half-brother from that marriage, though he was no longer legally bound to his father. Johnny moved to London with his new wife Betty and they lived there all the years that I remember, so you can see that my family roots were a tad unusual.

I always felt my parents were destined to meet and marry. Both had elements of the orphan Child Archetype and when they met in 1958, they fell in love quite fast and were married very young. My older sister was born in October 1961, twelve months after they wed and I was born in 1965, so by the age of 25, my Dad had achieved a new family and security! It was probably his dearest wish.

While we arranged my Dad's funeral, holiday brochures started to arrive mysteriously in the mail.

Come to Belfast and Northern Ireland they said and I found it curious to say the least. My Mum explained that due to my Dad's kidney failure, they had planned to go to Northern Ireland, as they had never been before. It was within the NHS too allowing my Dad access to medical care if he needed it.

On a bank holiday Monday, two weeks later, my Mum and I decided to book a trip to Northern Ireland as a break for us both. It was terra incognita. Neither of us had ever been and somehow it felt 'right' to go there, plus the brochures had been like a message from the divine for me.

Shortly after booking our trip, my Grandfather (my Mum's father who adopted her at age three) passed on aged 95. He left the planet, peacefully and in his own bed in a nursing home. He died as he had lived a very natural death with no need for pain relief or oxygen.

I could sense my life shifting massively with these events and the visit to Belfast became even more poignant for me. At last, I could say goodbye to Michael, and really lay that ghost to rest. It was time to get answers and boy was I ready for it!

I started writing this book in the midst of these events at a two-day writing workshop, just days before my grandfather's funeral on the 12th June.

So this is Belfast!

Sinking to my knees, I practically kissed the earth and thanked the gods I had made it here at last! I remembered the discussion nearly twenty years ago. "I cannot see me ever going to Belfast," I had said to Michael, "not with all the troubles." In addition, there was no real encouragement that he wanted me to come and I knew no one else in Belfast.

"Yes, I'm more likely to come to Glasgow," he said, sipping his drink.

"You will look me up if you come," I had said, gulping a little as I had realised that I wanted him to do this for me. He looked away and I wondered what he was really feeling right now. "Here, that's my address. Look me up if you come to Glasgow," I repeated.

He took the note from me and pushed it in his pocket without answering. Then he drew me the picture I had been badgering him about since we met. It was like a caricature of him, spiky hair and quirky looking. He had written *Don't you forget about me – Simple Minds*, next to it. That along with his birth date, were to be my only two remaining souvenirs all these years later. I had destroyed all pictures and anything that reminded me of him – much too painful to keep on this journey of healing – I couldn't exorcise those two factors though, and so the trip to Belfast felt like an exorcism for me from my past to lay his ghost to rest!

It was also a joint pilgrimage. My mother – who never knew her real father – was coming with me to visit the birthplace of the man who I had told my life story to twenty years previously. Perhaps Michael held the key or maybe he was just a red herring in it all. I was open and in surrender to whatever would be as we explored terra incognita. It felt like an adventure – my life purpose and mission to discover the truth! We went over in the boat from Troon and arrived in Belfast a few hours later.

Would I meet Michael again or was this the end of the line? Was it just dead men talking through me and time to put it all to bed?

Time to come full circle and release Karma?

Free to love each other or someone new, I mused!

The last time I had seen Michael was on the 16th July 1988. He was meant to go home on the evening of the 15th but his flight was delayed and it felt like we were granted a few more hours together!

After we had taken our mock marriage vows on the beach in the early hours of Wednesday 13th July, we went back to Michael's apartment. I was still in such a high state and felt ecstatic after my out of body experience. We consummated the vows and I felt happier than I ever have in my whole life. As I lay there trying to sleep I had the next part of my mystical experience. I was flying high above us and it felt like I was 'taken' somewhere else and shown what I needed to know. Exactly what that was I have no idea. I just know it was a very unusual, mystical experience that defied description and it was many many years later before I would gain any new insight into that!

By the time Michael was going home we really had no concrete plans to see each other and I just felt abandoned by it all – by Michael and by God.

The fact we now had an extra night together just felt like I may get some closure and insight before he left for Belfast. We had a really wild night together. It was fun and passionate and it felt like we were cramming all our energy and desire into a few short hours – almost like having a stay on our execution. It just felt very very intense between us and I knew he felt the same! This was no one-way street.

The next day, slightly hung-over and dazed, we woke up together and hugged. Then we made our way back to where his cousin and brother were waiting for the tourist coach to return to the airport.

We ordered some drinks at the bar. It was hot, dusty, and I felt weak due to lack of food and yet I didn't want to eat.

Songs played in the background. *Mary's Prayer* by Danny Wilson rang out and I asked Michael if he liked it. The lyrics rang in my head: "Blessed is the one who shares your power and your beauty... Blessed is the millionaire who shares your wedding day."

"No!" he snapped; he didn't like it. It felt like he was withdrawing from me – his energy retracting – I could feel he was dreading our goodbye. He had never snapped like this before.

I shrugged it off and the next song was *All I Have to do is Dream* by The Everley Brothers. I sang it in my head: "When I need you in the night, when I need you to hold me tight, whenever I want you all I have to do is dream... dream!" It felt like a prophecy and I listened in awe to the song and prayed for guidance.

The voice that had been guiding me returned. "He'll come back... he'll find you," it said. "You have to let him go. He has other things to do first..."

I felt calmed by the voice and a great peace overtook me.

The next thing the coach had arrived and everyone who had been waiting for it moved towards it. We jumped up and walked to the middle of the small courtyard area. All eyes were on us.

I looked at Michael and could see the pain in his eyes.

"I hope you have a good life," he said gently, "you deserve it!"

I gazed back in horror! No words came. I couldn't believe my ears! I turned round without uttering a word and started walking away from him.

After walking about twenty yards, I had the sudden urge to look round at him, just one last time! But before I could, the voice barked at me, "Don't turn around."

I kept my eyes and head locked into a horizontal position aiming for the corner of the road. I knew I could turn there and be out of sight from all those onlookers and Michael, before I broke down. I walked briskly looking straight ahead. The hit song by Aswad was playing in my head "Don't Turn Around" and I was glad when I was out of sight. I dropped down onto the pavement and sat with my head in my hands. No tears came. I just felt like I was in shock and filled with utter disbelief at what had just transpired!

"We'll meet again, don't know where, don't know when, but I know we'll meet again one sunny day," the words from Vera Lynn's wartime song played through my head. It had been with me since childhood – this dream – and now it felt like the mystery around it was shifting into something new!

I wrote this poem to illustrate my feelings about it all:

Fate & Destiny!

What is this life?
Is it ordained or fated
Or are we free within certain boundaries

So many years have passed
Since my destiny was foretold to me
And still I seem no nearer to fulfilling it
Or am I?
Life is so strange and contradictory
Always challenging us when we least expect it
And beckoning us along with more
Questions but few answers
Am I really free to break through this chain
Of fate or freewill
Or am I just living another illusion

Does destiny mean "It has been written"
And if so, when or how is this so
Is all this struggle to no avail
If all we have to do is trust
And let go and let God

And why is it so easy

To read of others' fate
Than it is to live and accept our own
Unless it's a favourable prophecy
Oh what a tangled web we weave
Just in this one lifetime
Is it any wonder that Karma always comes around
Not to haunt us, just to balance the account
So here I am
Ready to accept my destiny
Whatever it may be from here on in
To serve and do God's Will
From now to forever
For I do believe the weaver of destiny
Has it all planned out
Well in advance of our birth
And we are each chosen
To play our small but vital part
In the royal road we walk
And fulfil our very own fate and destiny!

Destiny Calling

"The minute I heard my first love story I started looking for
you, not knowing how blind that was. Lovers don't finally meet
somewhere. They're in each other's souls all along" – Rumi

I loved to read horoscopes as a young girl and was so fascinated that my destiny might well be 'written in the stars'. One of my favourite authors – Catherine Cookson – was a great inspiration. I realised just how much her model of the world had impacted mine. She wrote with such flair, tapping into that heightened sense of destiny and the story unfolded almost like magic, as you knew it would. Interwoven connections between people and their moral dilemmas; unrequited love, ill-timed love affairs and illegitimate children merged with a backdrop of poverty, religion, snobbery and various types of prejudice. The obstacles, which centred around these themes, were often dramatically swept aside by the central characters –

who had aspirations well above their station! The hero/heroine made good and triumphed in spite of the restrictions!

Underpinning it all, she brought the truth to the surface in each book – the unwritten truth of the characters and the lives that many were doomed to experience until that moment when the date with destiny became a reality. Some might call it the spark of genius, inspirational knowing or a sense of calling when you wake up to who you truly are inside, and then all the obstacles in the world hold no match for the desire to follow and fulfil it! This is the hero's journey!

It all seemed to me back then that the stories of our lives are written long before they will unfold and predestination has always held a strong pull for me. The other area that held an equally important part of my attention was romantic love and relationships. I didn't go in for Mills and Boon – too sugary – but I did believe that we each had a soul mate, someone who could make life worth living and even if there was no actual sharing of that life in an everyday setting (far too mundane and dull to my romantic young mind) an unbreakable bond existed. Somehow, throughout all my childhood, teenage imaginings, secret desires and longings, I felt sure it would happen. And of course that's how it did indeed magically manifest in my reality – long before I had ever heard of the law of attraction!

Carl Jung would say it was inevitable-synchronicity to meet that which I dwelt upon and of course perception IS projection. So even if my picture of this as a young girl was hazy, when it happened it was crystal clear! I couldn't have written the story any better if I'd tried.

"What happens to a person is characteristic of him. He presents a pattern and all the pieces fit. One by one, as his life proceeds, they fall into place according to some predestined design." –Carl Jung

The key to my life has been astrology. Unveiling the symbols and codes hidden in my chart that would guide me out of the depths of despair many many times as I studied them and learned more about what the serious study of astrology can tell you – my mystery school was animated!

The film *The King's Speech* also illustrates how much 'they' seemed to know about their 'destiny' even before it unfolded. Of course, the film was made with the sure knowledge of how it did unfold, but the hints and obstacles stood out like giant markers.

The key is to pay attention, join the dots and understand the BIGGER picture of your life by following those hunches and inspirations. They occur to make you follow them – you are the creator – the actor and the narrator of your own drama!

Nothing happens by accident, we are meant to be in certain places and meet key people. It happens on purpose and to show you the next step of the path that is unfolding within you. These are dates with destiny!

In fact, until I cast my Sacred Contract and became more consciously aware of my life purpose in 2009, much of what had happened in Corfu was still very much a mystery!

After my Gran had passed on in May 2009, I had embarked on my new path to create my business. Now I had been running a business on a part-time basis for years – since 2003 but it just never seemed to get anywhere. Sure, I helped people and made some money but it was more like a hobby a very expensive hobby rather than a profitable business!

After my trip to Belfast to meet and work with millionaire mentor Bernadette Doyle, that same month I embarked on creating this new business and called it *Your Sacred Purpose*. Bernadette helped me to see how valuable the work I was doing could be for many people. I had been so unhappy in my job working for Atos Healthcare, I figured that I needed a savvy business mentor and, as things were unfolding with such speed now, the day job was top of my list for what had to go!

That August I had a trip organised to work in Bradford for Atos as one of their travelling practitioners; it was all expenses paid for travel and I was booked to stay in a very plush hotel.

My niece was studying English literature at the time at University and as part of our family coming together to heal, we arranged three days at Haworth – the home of the famous writing family – The Brontës. It was to be another turning point for me. I had always loved *Wuthering*

Heights and had read it aged eleven. It was so passionate and spoke to me of obsessive and passionate love – even of two souls who are truly one!

As Cathie says, "I am Heathcliff!" and that just spoke to my desire for my own soul mate at a young age. So whilst we visited the parsonage and I enjoyed a few days with my Mum, sister and niece, I felt that more revelations were unfolding around me.

My Mum had offered us all a choice of jewellery from my Gran's collection. I chose a few pieces including one ring that was particularly striking. It was Gold with three diamonds and four black sapphires across it. As I picked it up to claim it and made sure it fitted my finger, I noticed it had an inscription on it and two hearts either side of this. In the centre, it simply said 'Mum'. I was a bit taken aback; I thought I best check who had given it to my Gran, as it had this special engraving in it. It turned out that no one knew where it came from or who gave it to her.

I had laid claim to it and it was at Haworth that my Mum gave it to me. Whether it was this or just the culmination of so many shifts going on within me I'll probably never know; however, I had a mini nervous breakdown in August 2009, whilst carrying out medicals in Bradford. The final straw was when one of the claimants came in 'wearing' something called a 'halo frame'. He had nearly broken his neck and this was in place as a form of support. It felt like a sign – a sign to move on! I ended up off sick from my 'day job' for the next four weeks and ultimately handed in my notice to Atos. I was living in fear of losing my sanity and felt as if I was hanging on by my fingernails to 'normal' life!

Then I was guided to read this:

> *These spiritual states have a particular effect on memory. The force, intensity and meaning of what is experienced in the depths of our being ensure they are never forgotten. In essence, they are our remembrance of Him (God). They are imprinted, almost burnt on the soul permanently, and seem to be accessible very quickly if we turn our attention to His unforgettable imprint on our soul.*

These divine locutions† leave us so convinced of their truth that, although their fulfilment sometimes seems utterly impossible and we vacillate and doubt about them, there remains in the soul a certainty of their verity, which cannot be destroyed. Perhaps everything may seem to militate against what was heard and years pass by, yet the spirit never loses its belief that God will make use of means unknown to men for their purpose, and that finally what was foretold must surely happen; as indeed it does. Teresa of Avila. ‡

So I left my old life well behind and embarked on my new one in 2010! This was to be the year that I would change my name back to my maiden name; I would go through another dark night of the soul, join *Damsels in Success* in Edinburgh and do a course called Calling in the One.

However, I am getting ahead of myself!

From adversity to fulfilment

Every adversity, every failure, every heartache carries
with it the seed of an equal or greater benefit.

Life can be difficult at times and we all have to meet and deal with adversity in life. As Kipling infers: *"Great is the person who meets triumph and disaster equally without the need to favour either."* Perhaps like me you have had to face up to a myriad of difficulties and adversity so great that you have questioned everything – a bit like the dark night of the soul as described by the mystic St John of the Cross. Here I was again just as I had been in 1998 and 2003. This time I decided to risk it all for love and see where it took me!

I was 44 years old, divorced, no kids, close to broke and with no regular income or job, I was living the life of a semi-recluse! I had been abandoned

---

† Locutions represent a voice from the deepest part of our heart, rising and emerging to give us advice or to keep us on the spiritual track. The main characteristics of true locutions are their strength, their sincerity and the ability of the message to bring a sense of relief, peace and comfort *Towards Mystical Union* by Julienne McLean

‡ *Towards Mystical Union* by Julienne McLean page 287 – from Mansion 6 of *The interior Castle* by St Teresa of Avila:

by some of my peers who had taken it upon themselves to exclude me from their group and the work we had been doing together.

I took it as a sign to move on and to seek out support elsewhere. It hurt, just as the rejection from the man who had been a catalyst for my marriage breakdown and who had rejected me while marrying his girlfriend and having a child with her, hurt. I just believed there had to be a reason for it all – one that I may not even be able to imagine right at this point in my life! It did occur to me that I was being protected – that maybe Michael would come back – but more than that I just came to equate Michael (and all that he stood for)with God, as that is what the name Mi-Ka-El in Hebrew means: "Who is as God".

It seemed to me that whenever he showed up in my world it was really God protecting me – as Caroline Myss often says: *"Man's rejection is God's protection."* I knew there was something in that!

So with my house sold, career non-existent and friends scattered to the four winds, I was asking questions once again.

Who am I? Where is God in all of this mess! I was seeking the perfection of my mission and this time I was not prepared to leave without new answers!

I knew that I had had a strange life – not your normal by the average standards; Extraordinary YES – but not in a good way!

It had been a challenging life like living in a dream – never dull; sometimes boring – but never, ever dull! Since experiencing this inner knowing in 1998 that God is always nearby and divine surprise is but a heartbeat away, I had began living a life of trusting that even the darkest moments will take me the distance and God will carry me through – no matter what!

My childhood dreams?

Simple; happy marriage to my soul mate, to serve God and have children!

Really, that was it; too much to ask or just that my ambition was never allowed to breathe or given free reign.

It has been one hell of a journey and not all rainbows that's for sure. However, if you asked me to exchange it for a normal average life and take away all the amazing miracles and divine inspirations that I have experienced, I would have to say no. There are two reasons I say that.

Firstly, what I have learned has been worth the exchange this far at any rate and taught me that healing myself was more important than creating a child that may have had to carry my shadow or fulfil my unlived potential. I always wanted to have children when I was younger but only if I was healthy and able to be a conscious parent who knew how to give. I never wanted to create a child as some kind of crutch or consolation prize for my unfulfilled life. I saw too many of my peers sacrifice their potential and live their lives vicariously through their children.

I wanted to be who I was first, and then, once I healed myself I would be able to create a child for the right reason; to give them the gift of life to enjoy and love them unconditionally for who they are. Of course, I do not condemn anyone for the former reasons and see that many people do realise that having children does not work out the way they planned anyway. Moreover, so often children are born through unconscious desires and selfish actions before people are conscious of who they are.

I was just determined from a young age that I knew better! I did not want to create more suffering for anyone. My main aim was to end my own and others' suffering even if that meant facing it head on without distractions. I always hoped though that I would have a child and it has been something that has driven my life forward and encouraged me to heal myself! I know many of my friends who have had similar challenges. So who knows; maybe there is still time for us all in the new world that is waking up!

Hand Analysis as part of life purpose

I decided to get my hand analysed on April 14th 2010, by life purpose expert Baeth Davis. I felt I needed some fresh insights and answers. I told her I felt stuck and that the same issue around relationships seemed to repeat. I was trying to get out of the triangle with the married man – though I was NOT having an affair at any point with him or anyone else.

0

I simply wanted to be with the 'one' and to be of service to God and the world – if that was on the cards and possible.

So Baeth told me that I had a cup of tears in both of my hands – meaning that my palms had a concave depression and that these symbolically hold emotion, tears and grief! My hands showed I was very sensitive and empathic and lightened the load for many others by doing so. Writing this book was important as I have lines of genius on both hands and by keeping so much bottled up inside that needed to be expressed, I would be unable to move forward. My hands also showed I was a gifted healer. My main purpose showed up as the creative innovator. I was a trailblazer who was here to bring through new information and writing this book was part of it all. As so much of my life purpose and destiny had been connected with my Gran, I felt it was important to share this message with the world.

However, the journey between April 2010 and then has been so pivotal in finding the answers for me that I had to include them here.

Next steps

MAY 2010
I attended a workshop with Bernadette Doyle in London in May 2010. I had just sold my home and the money was burning a hole in my pocket. I joined her LEAP programme with some of the revenue, as I felt it would teach me the skills that I perceived were lacking for me in the area of sales and marketing.

It was hard to shift from a job as a salaried nurse who didn't have to think of anything else other than care of my patients and keeping up to date professionally. Suddenly I was a proper business owner (not just giving sessions to clients when it suited me as I had been doing on a part time basis) and had to wear many hats to share my gifts with others.

As I had just sold my house, I no longer had anywhere to live. The day the offer came in, I texted some friends saying I had sold my house at last! I received two texts back that were like gifts from God – one from an ex-colleague at Atos said I could rent her flat as she was working in

England now and it was empty – the other said I could store my furniture in her garage. It felt like Divine Grace and that I was being supported in this big shift. I moved to Airdrie in June 2010 and what was left of my furniture went into storage. I sold quite a lot of my stuff and gave the rest away!

I spent four days on a writing retreat in St Andrews with three others and wrote some poetry along with notes for this book. It still felt too soon at that point to complete the book. I had no answers – just questions!

I was back in my cocoon feeling safe and nurtured. I wrote *Perfect Blue* on that retreat and it was my way of saying this is the end of the line of that old life!

Perfect Blue

Perfect blue
Bobbing waves
Sun high in the sky
And a boat appears
On the horizon like a spy
Catching the first breeze
A loosening of memories
Of days lost in the rain
Only peace rings in the soft air
A life renewed
The past relinquished
At long last
At long last
Goodbye

Baeth had recommended reading *Eat Pray Love – One Woman's Search for Everything*. It is the famous spiritual memoir by Elizabeth Gilbert and she felt it would guide me on my own adventure of finding the answers and for writing my own book – my own spiritual memoir. Therefore, I bought it and began reading it as I settled into the new flat. The first quote simply said: "Tell the truth, tell the truth, tell the truth" – Sheryl

Louise Moller. It was to become my mantra thereafter! I set up my business under my new mentor and set about creating programmes for new clients. The next four months in Airdrie, I followed the instructions of two postcards that were on the wall in my new bedroom. As the flat was fully furnished, it had given me quite a stir to see them. *Love* in silver blocks was emblazoned along the chest of drawers and behind the bed, it said the following:

Go for long walks

Indulge in hot baths

Question your assumptions

Be kind to yourself

Live for the moment

Loosen up, scream

Curse the world

Count your blessings

Just let go, just be

And

Dwell in possibility

I also had one last push to have a conversation with 'the other man'. Well it was the exact same outcome as it had been every time I tried to get an answer or closure there. He wasn't interested and chose to deny he had any feelings for me and he remained well and truly married!

I moved on!

At last!

So I went for long walks and went into a semi retreat. I nurtured myself and spent a lot of time alone. I knew I was bringing the 29-year Saturn cycle to an end and that this healing was necessary for me to move on and to find my heart's desire!

As Louise Hay says: "It is safe to look within." There is nothing that is greater than who you are and everything that comes into your life is to help you become more whole, loving and joyful in the greatest sense of the words. In reality to fulfil your divine potential and be, all you can be in this lifetime is your highest purpose!

Where your treasure is, there too is your heart and passion.

I knew I needed to metaphorically run towards the fire to get to my penthouse where true purpose and fulfilment were waiting for me!

I launched my first group webinar in September 2010 called *Discover the Real You and Make Your Dreams Come True*. I had people sign up from Europe, USA and the UK so it was a moderate success and I felt like I had lift off!

After I finished reading, *Eat Pray Love* in October 2010 and feeling as though I was coming out of my semi-retreat phase, I heard about an intriguing on-line course called *Calling in the One!*

I listened into the call and signed up. It felt like it WAS time to meet my soul mate!

Damsels in Success

I then noticed that a group called *Damsels in Success* was starting in Edinburgh in November 2010. I had been aware of it through Facebook as I was friends with Dan Bradbury. We had never met but I had been on his mailing list since March 2009 and had nearly attended his Top Gun event in London. I didn't go as I was working that weekend with NHS 24. I was aware of the birth of his daughter Summer when I went to La Manga to do an NLP course called Liberator in June 2009. She was born with a diaphragmatic hernia and needed to have surgery.

As a sick children's nurse I knew what that was, as I had nursed babies with it years before!

Damsels in Success is a women's personal development group. The creator is Lucie Bradbury who had started the group in January 2008 and then rolled it out in the UK to seven more groups in the autumn of 2010!

I had even briefly contemplated going to the initial discovery day in August 2010, but having committed to leap I didn't go ahead. I had also noticed that she was friends with someone else I knew from Glasgow in the personal development field. Therefore, I booked my place and went along to the launch in Edinburgh on the 2nd November. With my Damsel Archetype showing up in the 10th house of my own Sacred Contract, it felt like serendipity and guidance from my soul.

I joined *Damsels in Success* that day and spoke to Lucie and Jen about setting up a group in Glasgow.

No one could have predicted what would happen next!

I felt so excited that Tuesday when I got home. I knew something had shifted internally and that this was all in alignment with spirit!

When I had cast my own Sacred Contract in March 2009, it had shown that my highest potential house (10th house) had the Damsel Archetype right up there at the top of the chart. At first this was no surprise to me (as it made complete sense) and then I thought well how am I ever going to fulfil my highest potential and be empowered with my Damsel waiting for her Knight in shining armour to come and save her. It left me in a bit of a stew. However, I have always known that NOTHING out there has any power over me (or you for that matter) and so a way would show up that would help me to actualise the Damsel in an empowered manner.

And hey presto, here we were in 2010 and what showed up in my world but *Damsels in Success*.

So I set up a competition for my clients to enter to win a free opportunity to cast their own Sacred Contract with me and had a dozen entries pretty quickly.

I chose one winner from the entrants and then proceeded to convert 100% of my clients who entered that day! Thus I went from having a fledgling business to a full-on international one, which then acquired VIP clients over the next six months and has continued to expand and prosper!

It was amazing and I was overjoyed!

Calling in the One

I also started the seven-week course for *Calling in the One* with Claire Zammit and Katherine Woodward Thomas. It was very intense and in-depth but I was determined to crack it!

I listened to all the weekly calls and followed through on the exercises. It felt like things were shifting big time in my life. I released the notion of who the 'one' might be and just focussed on my internal barriers that had prevented me from meeting and being with the 'one'.

Two things happened. The snow and blizzard conditions that arrived on the 1st of December meant that we hit Ice Age conditions for over four weeks. Many people were marooned in their homes including me. Whoever this 'one' was, was pretty powerful as I felt like Rapunzel captured in her tower!

The December Damsels' meeting for Edinburgh was cancelled due to the snow and then Jen became ill and subsequently resigned as a leader over Christmas. Therefore, I was the only *Damsel in Success* in Scotland for a while and my main point of contact was through the forum.

I did the final exercise for calling in the one on the 21st December just as the total lunar eclipse fell on the winter solstice.

I wrote this poem that night and prayed that the 'one' would show up soon!

Beloved!

Calling in the 'one' is the climax to this year
On the winter solstice and total lunar eclipse
To shine the light on our destiny

And each of us can move deeper into the light
Freed from the shadows
Embracing the divine plan
And knowing your Will for this life dear God
To make a wish for restoration and full knowledge of it are my
greatest wishes
So I open to hear the sweet music and let its melody
Play through me
Opening up
Heart centres
And
White as it is outside
I know the purity of this great time
Can infuse life with greater intensity
Than anything ever known previously
To love with abandon,
Unconditionally
True love
Freed from the need to make sense
Just to sit in awe and watch the sunset and know that
the next time
It rises
Somehow you will be closer to me
My beloved
The reason for being
The air that I breathe
And nothing else can ever replace you
It is everywhere and nowhere simultaneously
Love oh love divine
Seeking me out and bridging this gap
To take me to the next layer of pristine newness
Tingling with the anticipation
Of the moment
Our eyes meet and we merge fully as one
Nothing else can ever replace
You

Moments
Each moment we breathe
And never realise that
It is not given
For we may take for granted
That those most precious moments are
The ones we pass over
Not realising
It will never come again
To seek and search for what
That special still point
When we breathe in unison
With the Universe

How can it not be that we
Are so deeply cared for and loved
Even protected in our aloneness
A fractured heart that yearns to be healed
That saw its own demise
And awaits its resurrection
To fully open into the joy that you ignite
Within and around
How can anyone truly know what it is to
Have experienced a love of such cosmic intensity
That it lifted up
High into the sky
There you were
The joy and sorrow
That filled me
Oh Ella she was such a happy girl
Dancing home
Only wishing for the fulfilment
The moment when it would all come together
And there would be no more searching
Just the peace of love fulfilled and experienced
Like a great watershed

Each snowflake bows in reverence
The icicles stand tall in salute
The enchanted forest is ours
To be as one
No more loss
Ignite the light
And the rest will fall into place
Ready to show what we are worth
Love it's always been hidden inside
Time to shine that light forever more
The latent power of you!

When I woke up the next day my Google mail account had been hacked and it felt like a sign from the divine that I was ready for another big shift!

2011 arrived and I felt called to do another course called *Awakening to Your Life Purpose* by Jean Houston.

Then on Valentine's Day, I posted the love manifestation invocation (see resources in Chapter 4). Again things shifted! On the 9th April, I started Jean Houston's next course *Living your Supreme Destiny*. I felt like I was on an accelerated learning curve to say the least!

This business of finding answers and the 'one' was becoming fast and furious. Could I keep up?

I wrote this in my journal:

Everything is brighter and I feel energised and alive. Alive with my purpose and love for myself and my life. I can have my true love and highest destiny. It has been written!

Then I had a revelatory dream of the 'one' on the morning of the 10th of April. It felt like we were getting closer and the 'one' was different from what I was expecting. The three Archetypes that came from the dream were King, Teacher and Lover.

At *Damsels* around this time, I was involved in a writing project. It was to write a story, poem or piece of prose inspired by the novel *Half of a Yellow Sun*. I wrote mine on the 17th April 2011.

Half of my Yellow Sun

Distant memories rise up
Of days long since past
When the Sun was high in the sky
Hotter than July
An awakening at last!
How are you?
So very pleased to meet you
How did it all happen they mused
Was it a dream?
A vision yet to unfold?
Or just a mirage?
Only true love is real or so I'm told
Will the other half of the Sun show up to reflect what was lost
Or will it remain an unfinished tale
What to do when you are left hanging?
To a silver cord as it winds its way upwards
Reaching into the deepest pools of the furthest flung heavens
Only the right time and place allow an opening
The wound heals and frees us all
But from what?
From ancient history
This love of past times meets an uncertain future
And the desire to meet again
But what if there can be no more endings
And new beginnings emerge
Almost there
Better things coming our way
Renewal in this light
Freedom from all that was and ever will be
And resolution in knowing this

Let go and sink into the hot Sun
Ignite the switch
Divine Bliss
Keep moving into this light
Freed from the dark spaces
Lighting up the shade
The other half of the Sun emerges
And is opening into a new world
A brighter world
Full of hope, happiness and turning this world
Right ways up
The new view
Is here now!

I was filled with new hope and had agreed to attend a discovery day for recruiting new leaders for *Damsels in Success.*

One week before it was scheduled I was in London for a conference with Bernadette Doyle and client magnets.

I went out for dinner with seven others in a posh part of London near our hotel. Whilst chatting and drinking wine I felt something shift. I looked down to get my handbag and check my mobile phone. It wasn't there. I searched around and asked my friends if they had seen it. No one had! I felt a sickness in my stomach. I knew it had been stolen and that is how it turned out!

The CCTV cameras would show that two well-dressed men had come into the restaurant and been hanging around the door waiting for a seat.

When the staff approached them, they had said they were waiting for someone else. Once the staff moved away, they pulled the long strap of my handbag from under my chair along the floor and under their long coat and left! It was as simple as that. The irony of it was not lost on me. Two well-dressed men who were stealing my money, credit cards and mobile phone, were basically abusing my trust.

I knew that weekend that I had to move on and was grateful for *Damsels in Success!*

Damsels in Success Discovery day

I attended the Damsels' discovery day on 21st May 2011 The door was open in the boardroom it was being held at and it was empty. I was staying in The Holiday Inn across the road from this hotel and had arrived early. I was feeling especially happy and was sure it was going to be a good day!

I sat down and was joined by another prospective leader. We started chatting and the conversation turned to one of the talks I had listened to recently by a woman called Tara on women and motherhood. I couldn't quite remember her second name and was racking my brain when Dan Bradbury appeared and reminded me it was Green! We had some introductions and then Lucie and the other prospective candidates arrived.

I was chosen to be one of the leaders with four others and felt excited by the prospect. Another piece of my life purpose puzzle fell into place and my Damsel in her 10th house was now in her element – ready to light up Glasgow and the world!

The next few months were busy and intense. I was working with more clients, casting their Sacred Contracts and training as the leader for *Damsels in Success.*

Then we got the opportunity to work with Christina Morassi – the heart-shot photographer – as she was over in London for two weeks. Ten leaders of *Damsels in Success* and Lucie, all got together for the day. We met at The Sherlock Holmes Hotel in Baker Street and spent the morning opening up to our true radiance with Christina as our guide. We danced and sang and did lots of exercises together. Then we got changed into our dresses. It was so exciting to feel like we were "flipping our switches" as Christina put it.

We got loads of pictures taken in Regent's Park and I really felt like all the training and preparation I had been doing in 2011, come together and integrate that day.

The pictures of us individually and as a group were fantastic and I was over the moon! I would continue my association with Christina, as she became another mentor for me to support me in actualising more of my life purpose in form.

In fact, that whole Summer of 2011 was so fabulous, as so many of my dreams were coming true!

I wrote this on my blog post in September 2011.

> *It has been like a kind of magic since I had joined Damsels in Success and cast my own Sacred Contract! I have worked with an AMAZING mentor who is an expert in life purpose, Jean Houston. I have attracted VIP clients who want to do my higher value specialised programmes, been to London for a photo-shoot with the heart-shot photographer Christina Morassi, and sailed through Venice in a gondola. I met Gerard Butler (of PS I Love You fame and loads of other famous people at a charity football match I was collecting for through Oxfam) and enjoyed a cruise on the Thames with Dan Bradbury's platinum mastermind group. The list goes on and on of amazing moments – in fact, living my dreams!*

I launched *Damsels in Success* in Glasgow at Kudos in Waterloo Street, on 13th September 2011.

I had about 40 guests signed up for the launch with two days to go and everything was going really well.

The weekend before the launch, I had noticed that the hurricane that had caused havoc in USA was going to be over Glasgow and Scotland on the Tuesday.

On the day, the weather was horrific and getting worse by the hour. A few people called it off saying they couldn't make it. I had bought a cake, pink heart-shaped chocolates and a wire-shaped heart ornament with my motto Follow Your Heart on it.

As I got ready to go to the venue and put everything together, more people called it off. I started to get upset and eventually was so angry that anyone or anything thought they could stop me doing this that I had a full-blown tantrum!

When I arrived at the venue at Kudos, it was all set up and looked lovely. I felt much calmer!

Around twenty ladies showed up and I was glad that so many made it, as it really was like *The Wizard of Oz* outside by this time!

The launch event was called *Live the Dream* and it went well.

Damsels in Success Glasgow was birthed and the group grew over the next few months.

Twin Flames, Soul mates and Calling in the 'One'

I was still interested in discovering more about calling in the 'one'. I had also become interested in twin flames via a Facebook page.

The information explained that twin flames were coming back into unification and that the love between them transcended the limited consciousness of the three dimensional world we are encased in.

Liora puts it like this:

> *"The Sacred Twin Flame Reunion is a love that transcends the limited consciousness of duality. The highest state of human love is the unity of one soul in two bodies. The soul connection is a compelling magnetised vibration of sacred divine union. The intense yearning towards the other is a knowing that comes from the depth of the ONE soul. Your Beloved may be on the earth plane, yet when two individuals come together, there may be egoic reactions, even though you know you are true Twin Flames at soul. These 'relating' initiations are designed for the potent and required journey to inner wholeness of each Twin Flame. Some conflicts tend to be opportunities for deeper intimacy for these unique Divine Reunions. There is only ONE true Divine Counterpart. You have known each other from the beginning of time. You know you are in completion. This is the true quest for Wholeness at this time of Ascension. You feel complete yet have a deeper awak-*

ening upon Reuniting. You never felt this depth of connection before from a soul mate.

Beyond the challenges together, you know the connection is unfathomable. You know your soul is connected forever. You are a true gift to each other as well as the entire Universe. Your combined vibration is felt throughout the Cosmos for the Awakening of the Planet at this time of the Golden Age. The One soul already knows who she or he is in all their Aspects, for all their Aspects make up the One. You realise every circumstance and experience of your whole life led you to each other through synchronicity. All divinely orchestrated. Absolute Pure Magic.

The love of your soul, especially blended with your Beloved is beyond human dreams, is beyond human language, because as Twins, you are made from the essence of God. Twin Flames are the same soul signature/vibration. This Sacredness is beauty beyond compare.

Twin flames must have complete trust and faith that the Higher Power is working for their highest good, surrendering all worries, concerns and doubts. They are two bodies with one soul and one beating heart sharing in unconditional love. There is a great amount of initiations involved in the Reunion towards inner wholeness. Everything becomes exposed. As you mirror each other, you will know everything. You will be able to communicate telepathically. You have to be patient in knowing that you and your Twin Flame will be reunited in divine timing. There is nothing you can do to speed that up. As you complete and balance so does the planet on some level.

When Twin Flames unite, they unite as ONE under God. The way the Twins see each other, is the way that God and the Angels see each one of us. The bond between Twin Flames is beyond words and it is linked to their ONE soul. As you connect with and integrate the attributes and qualities of your other half, something magical happens – you return to wholeness within your own being, and you no longer look outside yourself for validation or for what you feel is missing.

It is this depth of Love that reminds them of the Oneness of Light to which they have returned to together... finally..."

This all fascinated me but I wasn't sure if I was any closer to actually being with the 'one'.

My Mum turned 70 on 11/11/11 and the whole family went to Edinburgh to celebrate. This auspicious date was also linked to a shift for Twin Flames coming into greater unity though I had no idea at the moment exactly how that might play out!

My *Damsels in Success* group was up and running in Glasgow and *Damsels* were having their first national conference at the end of November. The song *Firework* by Katy Perry was chosen and I had really loved that song, ever since I first heard it in November 2010! (This was when I started the "calling in the 'one'" and joined *Damsels in Success* – synchronicity again!)

At the *Ignite* conference I realised it was time to birth this book. I felt sure that this book had to be published on the 4th of July 2012, as this was my Gran's birthday. Related to my own birth chart, this was the most auspicious day too – lighting up my own destiny point – plus it is Independence Day! For me Independence Day on the 4th July 2012 is about being free of the past and being more of my sovereign self! I can step more fully into my own life purpose and be free of the past – completely! This book is both a celebration and a catharsis of my journey. It has been a cathartic experience to record and relive it and I would like to leave you with a letter from a goddess, which can help you to stay true to yourself and perhaps avoid some of the pitfalls I experienced along the way!

In doing so, just like Dorothy from the *Wizard of Oz*, you will step into your sovereign self and make new choices from a position of empowerment too! That is what mastering your destiny truly is.

Namaste!

Gill

Self-Discovery

Letter from a Goddess

My Dear friend,

Greetings!

The time is now right for you to know how very much I love you and see your true divine beauty. I know that as a woman/man you are aware of the vanities and material status that is hankered after. And that's OK.

However, I am here to remind you that deep within you is your very own treasure trove filled with gifts yet to be opened. These gifts are available to you as you journey through life and, when you ask for guidance and support, these are uniquely yours.

Each gift is represented by a jewel.

The first jewel is to love and honour your life and path. It will light up whenever you go within and pray as it comes from the beloved source of all that is. All you need do is ask for direction and be open to the signposts that will show up.

The second jewel is to see the sacred beauty that lies within all things. This will make each moment of your life a divine surprise and unfold the mystery of so much more – untapped beauty and wonder filled delights. It will light up when you stop and pay attention and appreciate what surrounds you now and in each moment.

The third jewel is to listen to the rhythm of your life, know when it is time to move on, and time to let go. This jewel will light up when you feel empty or alone. It is a signal that you need to release what is no longer working in your life or has completed its time with you.

The fourth jewel is to know yourself; every nook and cranny of what makes you tick, and who you truly are. It is the most prized of all jewels because as you know your true self, you will transform your own life, and all those you meet.

This jewel will light up more and more brightly whenever you ask the question – "What is my purpose?" – and you will know that this brings back much guidance in many ways that you can tap into. It calls forth your highest potential and is your special gift that you share with all. You cannot keep this to yourself for it will only cause you pain to know it is within and unlit.

I want you to light up each jewel now and know that the great Sun, which is the source of all light and energy, can keep them safe for you now. As you need to tap into these jewels and feel their light unfold, so will your life and destiny be called forth and the wonder of you will be born in a new and beautiful pattern. The golden thread that links you with all beings will be the route to light the path.

You are an amazing, loving being, and are here to love; be true to yourself and your own life and all will be very well.

From the Goddess of Love.

RESOURCES AND RECOMMENDATIONS

Below are my top ten recommended resources to support you in living your sacred purpose. I have listed them in the order I read them to take you on a grand journey of knowing the real you!

Exploring the 'inner you':

☞ ***Birth chart analysis*** – you need your date, time (if known) and place of birth. You can purchase an inexpensive computerised one or have an in depth consultation. This is the starting off point to understanding what makes you tick, the blueprint for your life, Karmic influences and the best insider guide EVER!

☞ ***Relating*** by Liz Greene – another great resource for all budding astrologers or just the plain curious, who only know a little but want to know much more! Brilliant!

☞ ***Be Your Own Counsellor*** by Sheila Dainow – a fabulous book with great exercises including 'understand your life script'. You will transform your life using this little gem, go at your own pace and dip in and out. Either way you will gain much insider knowledge and enjoy the journey she takes you on to understand yourself better!

☞ ***The Gateless Gate*** by Dick Sutphen – release your limiting beliefs with this great guided meditation CD. There is a ton of valuable information here and you can listen again and again. This is a MUST! The *Get enlightened fast* CD, as you take your very own virtual reality journey to the source of your being!

☞ ***You Can Heal Your Life*** by Louise L Hay – the must have self-help book to help you get out of your own way and start creating better health, more money and less stress. Forgiveness exercises, mirror work and affirmations help you to DO something that WILL work!

☞ ***Living with Joy*** by Sanaya Roman – a great book that is channelled, and comes directly from spirit guide Orin. It will guide you to a better understanding of how you can make your life more joyful, and not get hung up on the negative stuff! Increase your sense of aliveness and well-being as you open your heart. A nurturing guide to discover your life purpose!

☞ ***Conversations with God*** by Neale Donald Walsch – this is a fantastic series that will transform your life and any feelings of helplessness into hope, purpose and joy! An inner journey to examine how to create a better life with God as your companion!

☞ ***The Celestine Prophecy*** by James Redfield – way ahead of its time when written and still very enlightening. Read it and you will discover more about your life purpose, your role in the Universe and how to release what's blocking you!

☞ ***Sacred Contracts*** by Caroline Myss – visionary and practical – the must have guide. Read this and then contact an Archetypal Consultant to cast your Sacred Contract and shift your life from fate to destiny!

☞ ***The 28 Laws of Attraction*** by Thomas J Leonard – a great book, which takes the laws of attraction and REALLY REALLY explains them. Forget *The Secret* – this is for the more discerning person who wants to think a bit more deeply, understand what their life is truly about, how to attract all the resources required, and the best mindset for success much more easily!

Finding new Answers

Here is an exercise to find your own answers; it is about listing the main events in your life that have brought you to now. It can often help to join the dots and open the way for wisdom and insights to show up in your life and illuminate more of your true self and purpose!

☞ I have come to see 2012 and beyond as the years that truth and love WILL become a way of life on planet Earth!

"I believe that too often we collude to keep things suppressed in the collective as well as individually due to 101 reasons. It really is becoming clear that suffering occurs more due to repression than any other reason!"

I have been working with many clients recently; most of them actually do know their life purpose or have a sense/inkling of it (even before they signed up for any of my courses or programmes!).

☞ Most of them are looking for the guidance and support to live it on a higher level or to release what fears or doubts they have about doing so and really being their True Self! More importantly, they want to live their best life; their supreme destiny NOW and I guide them in that direction, as that has been my desire for as long as I can remember too... but also been my greatest fear if I am perfectly honest!

The myth that I often hear from those people I meet is this:

I know my life purpose!

The assumption being that somehow they do not need to explore it further or what they are doing is good enough for now!

What has become apparent to me is that I knew or at least had inklings of my life purpose from a very early age. The reasons I have studied a lot of the material from this genre seems to have been more around confirmation of it and to support my journey to fulfilling that innate potential, and that is what I give to my clients, who do know it at an intrinsic level too. It is in your DNA for goodness' sake!

Another way to say this is that it is a lot like breathing. You know how to breathe because you are breathing; it's natural and you wouldn't know how to stop (without ending your life) or want to for that matter – would you?! However, you may choose to do a course on breathing techniques or meditate on the breath to raise your awareness of it. You were always breathing though – were you not? Right – it is the same analogy as life purpose – the more you explore it, and there are many methods and schools of learning. The more you come to know yourself and live it from a higher level – The Supreme Destiny Level as Jean Houston calls it, as opposed to the Schlock Level, which is pretty crap!

For the sake of clarity and brevity, here is my 'very brief biography on my life purpose' up to now – April 2012! I can say hand on heart that it is the truth! I recommend doing something similar to gain clarity and insight for you!

Between the ages of five and ten I went to church with my parents. I asked my Mum if ladies could be ministers as I wanted to be one when I grew up. She said they could. At this time, Andrew Heron and William Barclay exposed me to the work. I noticed a post recently by one of my friends and clients (on Facebook) who cast her Sacred Contract with me earlier this year.

"There are two great days in a person's life – the day we are born and the day we discover why." – William Barclay Scottish Theologian and author 1907–1978.

I was fascinated by astrology as a child and wanted to understand the planets and, more importantly, how they influenced us and our lives.

DECEMBER 1986 – I bought a book called Cast Your Own Horoscope.

1988 – I saw a programme on TV about astrology and went to the Astrology Centre in St Stephen's Street Edinburgh. I bought my first computerised analysis of my birth chart based on my date, time and place of birth. It was very accurate and whetted my appetite for more!

MAY 1988 – I moved to Glasgow after months of depression (a dark night of the soul experience) and joined the astrology group at The Theosophical Society, Queen's Crescent, in May 1988.

JUNE 1988 – I had a hepatitis B injection as part of my health screening and to protect me as a sick children's nurse. It made me ill and due to this, I subsequently had ongoing health problems for years.

JULY 1988 – I went to Corfu on holiday, fell in love with a guy from Belfast called Michael (holiday romance) and had a mystical experience with him. I also started receiving direct guidance from my soul and guides after it (i.e. I heard voices telling me what to do – and no I was not crazy!).

SEPTEMBER 1988 – I began classes in astrology at the Theosophical Society with Elise Allan and have studied and worked with it EVER since!

SEPTEMBER 1989 – I got married to my boyfriend of four years on 8/9/89.

SEPTEMBER 1990 – I went to Nepal with my husband and did VSO. I also bought and read numerous books on Buddhism, astrology and spirituality that I would never have seen had I not went to such a mystical country. I was tikkared (blessed) by a holy man in Durbar square.

1991–1992 – I had health problems related to the aforementioned hep B along with various tropical diseases picked up whilst in Nepal and was subsequently diagnosed with M.E./CFS or possible MS at the Neurological Institute, Southern General Hospital, Glasgow (aged 25) after having scans and being an inpatient for a week.

AUGUST 1992 – I moved to Dundee and met Gary Kidgell, who was studying soul-centred astrology. He taught me this system and gave me a great deal of fabulous information related to the mystery schools. I didn't work at this time due to illness, so for me I was in my mystery school exploring what my life and purpose was all about (please note I knew a lot by this time but it just wasn't happening – according to me anyway!!). Illness being part of one's Dharma was not that attractive to me then! I started doing astrology readings for private clients, who paid me and returned for more!

1998 – I had a Kundalini Awakening experience whilst having cranio sacral therapy. I was also reading Caroline Myss's book *Why People Don't Heal and How they Can* at the same time – synchronicity!

1999–2000 – I did a LOT of healing work on myself and subsequently studied The 7 Rays – Transforming with Divine Will by Orin/Sanaya Roman in May 2000. I met a healer in Feb 2000 and had Shen/Kairos with significant shifts in my health and more insights as to why I had been ill and what had been repressed.

DECEMBER 2000 – I moved to Kilmarnock and my husband and I bought a brand new three-bedroom semi-detached house with three bathrooms – my health radically improved.

MARCH 2001 – I enrolled on a course called The Essential Healing Course – a twelve-month programme for healing. I studied NLP with Jonathan Clark and Touch for Health with Stan Giles on the course. I decided I wanted to learn more and became a practitioner of NLP and Master practitioner of NLP in 2003.

2002 – I read *Sacred Contracts* by Caroline Myss.

JUNE 2003 – I set up my own private practice and began seeing clients immediately.

DECEMBER 2003 – I left my husband of fourteen years.

MARCH 2004 – I returned to my job as a nurse, as I felt unable to support myself financially and still had some ongoing health problems – so for me this was the best solution.

2003–2008 – I studied Hawaiian huna, led workshops for women (inspiring women) and taught the 7 Rays course to a group of twenty students. I continued with my private practice, met Caroline Myss, and did her Fate to Destiny course at Findhorn (2006) and Entering the Castle course (2007) at Turnberry. I then got divorced, bought a new house on my own and generally lived my life.

MAY 2008 – My Dad passed on.

JUNE 2008 – I went to a writing workshop in Edinburgh with Tom Evans, run by Jackie Walker and started writing this book, which I called Sacred Paths Entwined.

JUNE 2008 – My Granddad passed on (four weeks after my Dad). My Mum and I went on holiday to Belfast to have a break from funerals!

SEPTEMBER 2008 – I started a job doing medicals for Atos healthcare and subsequently found that I hated it!

JANUARY 2009 – I decided to cast my Sacred Contract and signed up for the course with Caroline Myss. I also left my job and created Your Sacred Purpose as a brand (after working with Bernadette Doyle who I met in Belfast, May 2009) to bring together all of the above and share more fully with clients! I became a Certified Archetypal Consultant (with CMED-Caroline Myss Education). I cast my first destiny wheel in October 2009 and watched Slumdog Millionaire as part 3 of our course, brought to us by Jim Curtin one of the course tutors (who had worked as an agent for Hollywood actors Patrick Swayze and John Travolta in his previous 'life').

NOVEMBER 2010 – I joined *Damsels in Success* (I have the Damsel Archetype in the 10th house of my Sacred Contract) and I knew it was my destiny to do so.

NOVEMBER 2010–JULY 2011 – I worked with Jean Houston on Living Your Supreme Destiny and Life Purpose courses as well as Katherine Woodward and Claire Zammit (on their Calling in the One course).

SEPTEMBER 2011 – I had been chosen to be the leader of *Damsels in Success* in Glasgow in May 2011 and launched the Glasgow group on 13/9/11.

NOVEMBER 2011 – I attended Ignite – the *Damsels in Success* national conference at The Crowne Plaza in Birmingham. I decided I needed to birth this book Sacred Paths Entwined and have it published on 4th July 2012.

OK, so you get the picture I hope.

My life purpose and destiny have been gradually coming into manifestation on a moment-to-moment basis. Not just because I chose to do all of the above courses but because I believe we need to be aware consciously of who we are and why we are doing what we do – that is what living Your Sacred Purpose consciously is! That is the TRUTH!

Six essential keys to a more aware and spiritually developed life.

Here are the six essential keys to a more aware and spiritually developed life.

1. **Control of thoughts.** We must master our thoughts, particularly our train of thought. Just consider the way thoughts whirl about in our souls, how they flit like will-o'-the-wisps. One impression arises here, another there, and each changes our thinking. It is not true that we govern our thoughts; our thoughts govern us completely. We must reach the point where, at a given time in the day, we can become so absorbed in a thought that no other thought can enter and disturb our soul. In this way, we hold the reins of thought for a while.

2. **Control of our actions.** Here it is necessary, occasionally at least, to act in ways that are not precipitated by anything external. Whatever is initiated by our place in life, our profession, or our situation, does not lead more deeply into higher life. Higher life depends upon such intimate matters as one's resolve to do something that springs completely from one's own initiative – even if it is something absolutely insignificant. No other actions contribute anything to the higher life.

3. **Equanimity.** People fluctuate back and forth between joy and sorrow. Thus, we allow ourselves to be rocked on the waves of life. We must reach equanimity and steadiness. One must become steadfast and even-tempered.

4. **Understand every being.** Nothing expresses more beautifully, what it means to understand every being than the legend passed down to us by a Persian story. Jesus was crossing a field with his disciples, when they encountered the horrible-looking decaying corpse of a dog. Jesus stopped and looked at it with admiration, saying, "What beautiful teeth this animal has!" Within the ugly, Jesus found an element of beauty. Try always to approach what is wonderful in every phenomenon of outer reality. You will see that everything contains an aspect that can be affirmed.

5. **Complete openness**. Most people judge new things according to the old things they already know. However, we must not confront a new communication immediately with our own opinion. We must instead always remain alert for the possibility of learning something new. We must develop the ability to listen, because it enables us to encounter matters with the greatest possible openness.

6. **Inner harmony**. We receive this after we have developed the first five keys. Those who have the other qualities are also inwardly harmonious.

All things are possible – God alone suffices – Teresa of Avila

NB: Information related to Archetypes comes from CMED course on *Sacred Contracts* by Caroline Myss and the book *Sacred Contracts*.

Books related to chapter 7

The Kundalini Experience by Lee Sannella

Eat Pray Love by Elizabeth Gilbert

The Forces of Destiny by Penny Thornton

The Astrology of Self Discovery by Tracy Marks

A Path with Heart by Jack Kornfield

Calling in the One by Katharine Woodward Thomas

Twin Flames

The SACRED Twin Flame Reunion & Ascension

www.twinflame1111.com

LIORA Spiritual Teacher

ABOUT GILL

Gill Potter is the founder of *Your Sacred Purpose*.

Her background before entering the personal development field was in nursing and she is an experienced Registered General Nurse (RGN) and Children's Nurse (RSCN). Gill started off working life as a nurse mainly because she had a strong desire to help other people and on leaving school this was her chosen career path.

Gill was guided to go to Chicago to study Sacred Contracts with Caroline Myss. She cast her own Sacred Contract and Fate to Destiny Wheel in 2009 and this all ignited a new level of much higher awareness, amazing synchronicities and brought many new opportunities to her. She left nursing to follow her own calling in 2010 and has been having a ball ever since!

Gill Potter is an Archetypal Consultant as well as a Master Practitioner in NLP, Certified Time line Therapist and an astrologer. She now works with clients all over the world who want to know more about their sacred path and purpose. She is able to guide them using her in-depth knowledge of both orthodox and soul-centred astrology, which she has studied for many years, Sacred Contracts work and transformational coaching.

Gill also offers webinar classes, seminars and has her own radio show.

Some of Gill's recent work has included the following workshops:

> *Inspiring Women*
> *Passion and Purpose for all Inspiring Women*
> *Life Path Predictions*
> *Tune into your Moon*
> *Discover the REAL YOU and Make Your Dreams Come True*
> *Manifesting with the Moon*

Your Sacred Purpose was created to share everything that Gill has learned on her own path to know the divine and her own purpose. She now works with heart-centred entrepreneurs to support them and their business to grow exponentially aligned with their spirit. She inspires others to follow their true calling now.

GILL POTTER

Archetypal Consultant
and astrologer

info@yoursacredpurpose.com

www.yoursacredpurpose.com

www.joyfulsteps.com

Lightning Source UK Ltd.
Milton Keynes UK
UKOW040742220612

194853UK00001B/5/P